Keith Hill is a New Zealand writer whose work explores the intersection of mysticism, history, science, religion and psychology. His books include *The God Revolution*, *Striving To Be Human*, and *Practical Spirituality*, each of which won the Ashton Wylie Award, New Zealand's premiere prize for spiritual writing. Since 2008 he has been working with channeller Peter Calvert to present a new metaphysical perspective relevant to twenty-first century spiritual seekers. Keith's most recent books are *The New Mysticism* and *Practical Spirituality*.

Reviews of *The God Revolution*

"Hill's exposition is a fine example of scrupulously rigorous scholarship – it is remarkable how much ground is covered within his brief historical survey. … An impressive and accessible introduction to a challenging philosophical topic. " – Kirkus Review

"Keith Hill is a writer in the vein of Karen Armstrong … The prize that celebrates New Zealand's forward thinkers is thoroughly deserved." – Mike Alexander, Sunday Star Times

"A scholarly yet accessible book. … Deserves to be read by all those who care about ideas, the trajectory of civilization and its future form." – Peter Dornauf, www.eyecontact.com

BOOKS BY KEITH HILL

CHANNELLED BOOKS
What is Really Going On?
Experimental Spirituality
Practical Spirituality
Psychological Spirituality

NON-FICTION
The New Mysticism
The God Revolution
Striving to Be Human

FICTION
The Ecstasy of Cabeza de Vaca
Puck of the Starways
Blue Kisses

MYSTICAL POETRY
The Bhagavad Gita: A New Poetic Version
Walking Without Feet:
Selected Poetry of Mirabai and Kabir
Psalms of Exile and Return

CHANNELLED WITH PETER CALVERT
The Matapaua Conversations
The Kosmic Web

Where Do I Go When I Meditate?

Taking your meditation
practice to the next level

Keith Hill

attar‖books

First published by Attar Books 2018

The moral rights of the author have been asserted.

Paperback ISBN 978-0-9951059-3-5
Ebook ISBN 978-0-9951059-4-2

Cover designed by Abigail Kerr

Attar Books
www.attarbooks.com   www.experimentalspirituality.net

Contents

Using meditation
for spiritual enquiry

For a long time I had no idea just how multi-purpose meditation can be. My initial training, which goes back to the 1970s, involved using meditation in just two ways. First I was taught how to still the thoughts that constantly stream through our mind—the monkey mind, as Buddhist meditators call it, because it grabs stimuli and chases the resulting thought associations wherever they lead. Second, meditation helped me contact my spiritual self, the part that transcends our everyday existence. Both strategies worked for me, and even led to a handful of profound mystical experiences.

So years of personal practice confirmed to me that meditation works. At the same time, I was aware that many other people used meditation differently, particularly to promote health, reduce stress and develop a calmer, less reactive psychological state. In recent years a mindfulness movement has helped many focus on and stay mindfully within the present moment.

This is all good. However, over the last decade I have increasingly become aware that this isn't all meditation can be used for. It can also be used for spiritual enquiry. Meditation can help us resolve whatever troubles us. It can help us find answers to problems and puzzles. In addition, meditative states can also enable us move our awareness beyond everyday physical reality to explore alternate perceptual realms, and even to encounter non-embodied beings.

All this is another step, a big step, beyond what I was taught all those years ago. This is the next level. It involves sustaining a passive-active balance, in which we keep our everyday self and its restless mind passive, yet at the same time we actively engage with and deliberately respond to stimuli that come from beyond our everyday awareness.

Discovering this next level has personally led me to many fascinating perceptions and insights. It has also resulted in me communicating with a group of spiritual identities who have completed their cycles of incarnation as human beings on this planet. They are now acting as guides, sharing what they have learned, a task I am now also committed to. This book is the fruit of our work together. It is the second in a series of channelled books that use the format of questions and answers to illuminate pivotal human issues. The first book, *What Is Really Going On?*, looked at reincarnation and a range of spiritual issues. This book is focused on meditation and its implications. While some topics overlap between books, each is designed to be a stand-alone read.

The information the guides offer in response to questions about meditation—questions asked by friends, by me, and sometimes suggested by the guides themselves—isn't just informative. It is transformative. The guides open up possibilities for meditation and what it can be used for that have the potential to take you to the next level of your spiritual practice. I hope you find their answers as compelling, delightful and down-to-earth as I did when working with them on this book.

Keith Hill, 8 November 2017

Question 1

What's the point of meditating?

Today meditating is widely seen as the thing to do. Some people claim meditation helps them de-stress. Others say it supports their body's health. Spiritually, meditation is said to lift our awareness out of our everyday obsessions so we can merge with something beyond us. From your perspective, what is the point of meditating?

THE GUIDES RESPOND:

We begin by welcoming this opportunity to again respond to questions regarding humanity's spiritual nature and the life situations with which you, as incarnated human beings, find yourselves grappling.

In the first book in this series we answered a range of general questions regarding the human situation. In trying to make sense of life and the often difficult situations human beings so often find themselves in, people have historically offered a wide range of explanations. Some are astute. Some are obtuse. Some are of little use. Some are somewhat crazed.

We put this light-heartedly, yet the perspectives people propose, and the remedies they offer to address life's difficulties, can have either illuminating or devastating impacts on those who assimilate what is said and apply them to their lives. As the intent behind this question reveals, people do so precisely because they're confused about some aspect of their life, or have issues to clarify or problems to resolve, yet are confronted by a diversity of possible answers and don't know how to tell which are appropriate.

Seeking an answer, people commonly adopt the perspectives they were brought up with or in which they are professionally trained. Alternatively, they may iconoclastically reject those perspectives and adopt others, perhaps diametrically opposed. Whichever course they take, their underlying assumption is that a simple solution to life's conundrums can be found, clarification will come, and whatever troubles them will be resolved.

This hope for simple solutions is understandable. However, as even a little experience makes clear, nothing in human life is simple. No aspect of the human situation is as straightforward as you would like. There are always underlying plans, intents and patterns, most of which remain unperceived. Furthermore, those plans, intents and patterns may play out smoothly, not quite be in sync, or may go majorly awry. And even when activities *do* go well, the final results may not be as anticipated—this applies even when everyone does their best and acts with the best intentions.

You can see this at play in work situations. Let's say a group is carrying out a joint task. Everyone knows what they have to do. But different people do things differently. One never fully completes any task, requiring others to step in and finish it. Another is capable of doing a good job but has time management issues, so rushes his work at the last minute. The result may be satisfactory, or not. One contributor is overwhelmed by non-work issues. Another is just plain sloppy. As a result, no matter how competently you perform your part of the task, the performance of others impacts on the final result.

This small example indicates the interlaced complexity of human life. That complexity, in turn, suggests why simple answers are so difficult to obtain. The human situation itself prevents it.

In this case, the question has been asked: What is the point of meditating? It is an apparently simple question. The complexity arises from the fact that different people are in different life situations and face different problems. As a result they require different solutions. And if they are each to use meditation as a tool to find their solution, then they need meditation to provide them with different things.

For those with ongoing health issues, meditation can be a helpful tool not just for de-stressing but for diagnosing what is physically going wrong with their body. If the problem has its roots in what happened during a prior life, then meditation can aid deep level diagnosis that you won't obtain in a doctor's office.

For those who have difficulty getting on with others, who can't sustain relationships, whose key relationships are fractious, or who ultimately don't like living with themselves, meditation can help them focus on something greater than their flawed and frustrating personality. Meditation can take them towards a deep affirmation that they are, at their core, far greater than their current limited self.

This aspect of the human situation is common. People often feel uncomfortable with aspects of themselves and their life. Many try to suppress their unease, sliding past the feeling that there is something fundamentally limited in the way they are living. The fact is that unease of any kind is useful. It is only when people feel that something is wrong, that something in them isn't working as it should, or that they could be doing much better, that they become motivated to change. This applies to external social conditions as much as to personal difficulties. First a problem is identified. Then it is analysed. A plan of action is conceived. And that plan is put into action. Meditation can certainly contribute to that process.

In this sense, meditation is a practical tool, just one in the toolkit you have at your disposal to adjust aspects of your life situation. Other tools include introspection, which involves pondering on parts of your life in order to understand all it involves, extracting large or small lessons from your life experiences, attending workshops to gain new insights and to develop new skills, reading when it is done to obtain new information, and consulting those who are more experienced and knowledgeable to gain fresh overviews and guidance to augment what you already know.

These are all tools for growth. So using meditation as a tool for growth is certainly an application we recommend. But it is not essential. To speak in the context of solving life problems and facilitating personal growth, meditation is a useful tool, but it is not necessarily the best tool for the job. When you initially address a difficulty other tools might be more appropriate. Reading around the topic, attending a talk or workshop on a relevant issue, consulting an expert ... these may be more appropriate starting points. They are certainly often more effective during the early stages of problem solving. Why? Because they are straightforward means for obtaining the information you require to identify what is going on and plan what to do about it.

What about meditation, then? Does this mean it isn't straightforward? That it isn't a recommended means for obtaining insights and information? Our response is, it is. And it isn't.

This may strike you as a strange response. Why are we being equivocal when we initiated this series of question and answer books, and especially given we selected the topic of meditation for this book? We reiterate, the simple truth is ... the topic isn't simple. This is precisely why we have selected it.

Human awareness is layered. Your everyday awareness is caught up in and engrossed by the circumstances of your everyday existence. This is natural. It is why you, as a spiritual identity, chose to be born into a body. Incarnation offers an opportunity to have intense experiences, to extract lessons from those experiences, to develop skills to cope with the many kinds of experiences available within the human situation, and to learn to perform effectively. All this activity contributes to your evolution as a spiritual identity.

Behind each individual human life, behind your life now, is a spiritual identity that, to use conventional metaphysical language, transcends your everyday personality. Your spiritual identity transcends the human identity you consider yourself to be. This means that behind you is another you, and that other you is more knowledgeable, more compassionate, more loving, and has far wider and deeper perceptions, than you currently do as a human being. One point of meditation is that it provides a bridge between your *human you* and your transcendent *spiritual you*.

Is one *you* better than the other? No. Your human you is a creation of your spiritual you. Your human you is a manifestation of skills, traits and talents that you have gathered throughout all your prior lives. Your current human you is the next phase in your development of mastery in those areas of human culture that you have chosen to experientially explore this time round.

As such you, in the form of your current human you, are as necessary to the growth of your spiritual you as a sapling is necessary to the growth of a tree. A tree doesn't grow from seed to tree without going through the stage of being a sapling. The sapling stage is not inferior to the mature tree. Seed, sapling, tree: each is a necessary stage of growth. Similarly, you may view your human you as a sapling that is necessary to your growth into a mature tree. Of course, where the analogy breaks down is that a tree has just one sapling, whereas throughout the course of all its incarnations your spiritual you will select, plant and grow a thousand or so saplings. The eventual mature spiritual you will incorporate all these saplings. Moreover, your tree will add to a forest containing perhaps a thousand trees. This forest of collected identities will contain much knowledge, love and wisdom.

Meditation is a means for sustaining contact with your transcendent collective spiritual identity. It also provides a way to contact the forest of other spiritual identities among whom you are growing. That there are advantages in doing so will be readily apparent.

Accordingly, we suggest that there are three major points to meditating. The first is that it is a tool for solving problems. Second, it offers a way for you to make contact with your spiritual you and learn more about your transcendent identity. Third, meditation opens up your awareness, facilitating contact with other spiritual identities beyond your own.

Question 2

You mean meditation reveals secret information?

So meditation has different outcomes. I can buy that. But your answer opens up a lot more questions. You talked about using meditation to contact the transcendent spiritual root of our identity. You also mentioned using meditation to obtain information. Are you referring to transcendent information? Supernatural information? Information about future events? Secret information? Does meditation involve ferreting out people's secrets? Ferreting out our own secrets? And where do the Akashic Records fit?

THE GUIDES RESPOND:

When people start out on their spiritual journey most think in somewhat grandiose terms. However, the secret to spiritual exploration—we use the word *secret* not because there is any great secret to spirituality, but because human beings so much enjoy thinking there are secrets to be uncovered—the secret is that the best place, in fact the only place, where you can start your spiritual exploration is where you are right now, in your present state of mind, living your current life.

So the information we are referring to isn't on a grand scale. It is information pertinent to your current life situation. Accordingly, rather than trying to peer into the past or future, and instead of speculating about hidden levels of the cosmos, and certainly instead of trying to delve into the Akashic Records, we suggest you bring it all back home and focus on the who, where, what and how of your current life and its circumstances.

We admit this is a somewhat humdrum reply to your question. It lacks the romance, the grandiose cosmic vision, that many religions offer, with their tales of travels into the heavens, their visions of angels, and their promise of meeting the Divine. In our defence we suggest that these are somewhat nebulous. Even if such things ever do happen, they will be far in your future. Effectively, they will occur at another time, in another world. Our point is that you are not currently living in any distant possible world, you are living in this world, here and now. Your pains and pleasures, confusions and illuminations, blindnesses and insights, problems and solutions, exist right where you are now, around you and within you. So the information we recommend you seek consists of information regarding your present life situation.

Information comes in many forms. We first draw your attention to psychological information. This involves extending your understanding of your own personal psychological make-up and those of your family, friends and colleagues with whom you live, work and play. This kind of information is crucial to working through the grating of personalities that is an inevitable aspect of human life. Often people grate with each other not because one or the other is a so-called bad person, but because their respective personalities contain incompatible elements. Understanding in depth the different aspects of other people's personalities, knowing which parts of your own personality to turn off when you interact with them, and learning how to do so, lies at the heart of psychological knowledge.

Another significant form of psychological information that contributes to your spiritual development consists of knowledge of your own habitual behaviours, how they arose, how they function within your overall psyche, how their impact may be diminished, and how to eventually eliminate those habitual behaviours that limit your growth.

Why does eliminating habitual behaviours help your spiritual progress? Because habitual behaviours lead you to respond to new information in old ingrained ways. If you possess psychological gloop—and everyone does—then whatever information you come across ends up getting processed into that same gloop. In order to progress you need to face up to ongoing behavioural issues, identify underlying problems, and initiate action plans to change how you do things. As the saying goes, you can't keep doing the same old things and expect to get new results. To rise out of your inner gloop you need to do, feel and think in new ways. New information provides what you require to begin to achieve this. Yet here we strike a conundrum.

Let's say you want to transform your old gloop-filled self into a more knowing, more loving, wiser self. Or maybe you're not that ambitious. Maybe you just want to do one thing in your life better than you have been. The situation is that your gloop-filled self has a string of habitual ways of feeling, thinking and doing. So even if you get new information that identifies the problem and provides guidance on how to work through it, your ingrained gloopy behaviours will process that information in their habitual ways, offering doubts, saying it won't work, and in the end turning the new information into the old familiar gloopy stuff. This is a chicken-egg scenario. You need new information to change, but you need to change in order to access and process that new information. The conundrum is you need to change in order to change.

What happens if you never absorb new information? Nothing much. Yet a solution exists that can dissolve the conundrum and lift you out of your gloop-filled self-limiting habitual behaviour. The solution is meditation. Meditation involves shutting down your gloop-filled self's thinking. That self engages in a continuous inner monologue. When you speak unthinkingly it is inevitably the gloop-filled self talking, expressing its habitual ways of feeling and thinking. Shutting down the constant flow of your gloop-filled inner monologue enables you to process whatever new information you receive in an equitable manner, free of the old self's agenda—which is to keep doing what it has always done.

Accordingly, sitting in meditation, with the mind of your ingrained gloopy self quiet, enables you to process new information however you receive it, whether via books, workshops, seminars or through obtaining expert guidance. Free of the ingrained self's habitual blaming, justifying, excusing and denying, you can evaluate the new information, relate it to your own life situation, use it to illuminate the dark corners of your gloopy self, decide how to change your life and, in the long run, transform yourself.

Sitting like this, inwardly quiet, has another significant outcome. It opens you up to other levels of information. This is because when you sit in silence you may start to hear voices that are not your own. We are not talking about schizophrenia, a psychotic state in which people hear voices—such as those of God, the Devil, or various deceased personalities—who tell them what to do. We certainly do not mean you will hear voices in this sense. Rather, we are using the word *voices* as a metaphor.

When inner silence is sustained over a period of time, a condition is generated in which you may begin to discern very quiet streams of thought. We call such a stream a voice, but it is not heard in a conventional aural sense. So when we say *a voice is heard by the ear of the mind* you must be aware that neither ear, voice nor hearing are literally involved. For example, this communication is reaching our scribe via a subtle stream of thought that he is aware does not come from him. To say *this communication involves him hearing a quiet voice coming from somewhere else* is a metaphorical and not a literal description.

Our scribe's ability is not special. Anyone can do it. It just takes a desire to do so, and a period spent in training learning to quieten the gloopy self's mind sufficiently to hear quiet and subtle voices that come from *out there*. At this point we wish to share a secret. This secret is the biggest secret in your life. The secret we wish to reveal is that the biggest secret in your life is ... you.

This statement may seem mere froth, to be just another piece of New Age faux wisdom. We sympathise with such a response. Nonetheless, we are not being facetious. We ask you to consider this statement in a quiet state, without your gloopy responses kicking in. Assuming you are in such a state as you read this, we repeat: The biggest secret in your life is you. The most important source of information is you. The most significant contributor to your growth and transformation is you.

In our answer to the previous question we drew a distinction between your current *human you* and your transcendent *spiritual you.* That spiritual you is your primary source for the information you need to grow. It knows more than you do because your spiritual you has lived many, many lives. In contrast, you in the form of your current human you only know this life. Accordingly, the voice of your spiritual you is the first subtle voice you need to hear. It can offer you sound insights and useful advice, given it has lived through similar (or even the same) situations as those you are going through now, and given it has an overview of all that is involved.

This voice can legitimately be called a secret because, in the midst of the conditions of ordinary life, it remains hidden. It may also be characterised as the pirates' mythical buried treasure, as the princess locked in the tower, as the alchemist's red sulphur, as the Philosopher's Stone, or as the Pearl of Great Price people spend their lives trying to obtain. The good news is that your spiritual you is not mythical. Nor do you have to sail to distant lands to find it. However, you do have to fight a dragon before you can access it. In the context of this discussion, the dragon consists of your gloop-filled self and its constant stream of self-limiting thoughts.

While we are in the realm of myths and legends, a Greek myth relates how a soul drinks from the river of Lethe just before it leaves the underworld and returns to the human world to be incarnated in its next body. Drinking the river Lethe's waters induces a state of forgetfulness, so when the soul is born in its new body it is unable to remember its previous lives, or indeed that before it was born it existed for an extended period in a non-embodied, spiritual state.

In the previous book in this series we stated that forgetfulness is necessary for reincarnation to function effectively, because each spirit needs to live unencumbered by memories of all its prior incarnations, especially the mistakes it made. Now we can add that what sustains the state of forgetfulness throughout your life is that you are constantly drinking from the stream of thoughts emanating from your gloop-filled self. This stream promotes forgetfulness because it keeps you involved in the minutiae of your current life. This involvement isn't at all a bad thing, given it lies at the heart of being human. You have to get involved in order to live a human existence and so be in a position to extract what being human offers. Yet there are other possibilities besides being forgetful for your entire life.

When you engage in sustained periods of silent meditation, one outcome is that you stop constantly drinking from your gloopy self's stream of thoughts. Inwardly free, you start to hear the quiet voice of your spiritual you. As contact is maintained, that quiet voice, at first heard intermittently, gradually becomes a stream of subtle thoughts. And as you drink from this alternative stream of thoughts you start to remember things, things that you at the level of your spiritual you know well, but that for you as a human you have long been hidden and secret. Meditation makes remembering possible. Remembering is the process of you as your current human you becoming aware of what you as a spiritual you already know. Remembering is the process of digging up the secret treasure of self-knowledge regarding who, what, where and how you are.

The question has been asked, what about other people? Can you access their buried secrets? Yes, certainly. You can gain insights into other people's psychological make-up and infer what past events, even those that happened in prior lives, have led to them manifesting their current habitual behaviours, their current levels of health, and their current personality.

Gaining insights into another's future is much more complex. Some insights into others' buried secrets can be obtained via meditation. However, this is a complicated topic that defies simple explanation. It is the case that some people choose to incarnate with the intention of using their so-called psychic abilities to help others. We are specifically referring to mediums who ferret out buried personal and family secrets as part of their work to help the non-embodied convey information to the embodied, whether to resolve issues caused by grating personalities or to dissolve grief. But you do not need to be a medium to ferret out others' secrets. Anyone who lives intimately with another for years is in a position to access their deepest secrets, entirely due to proximity allowing you to get to know them well. However, you only ever dig up another's buried secrets when you really wish to do so. The fact is that most people don't feel comfortable digging into anyone else's deepest secrets, given they have no desire to delve into their own.

We must also emphasise the role observation plays in obtaining insights into what drives others. Using data obtained via straightforward observation, it is quite possible to infer much about another person and their deepest motivations. However, in order to infer coherently you need to use an appropriate psychological framework to process your observations. One such framework developed for the modern outlook is offered by the Michael Teachings. Others have been developed historically within Buddhism, Jainism, Sufism, Taoism, Kabbalah, and other spiritual traditions. People also develop their own frameworks in the context of their experiences. They are all valid in their own ways, but of course none is full and complete because the mind of the embodied human you simply cannot encompass everything that is involved. Nonetheless, by using an appropriate psychological framework to process observations, a great deal more can be ferreted out and understood than is normal among human beings.

To conclude, we address the question of how the so-called Akashic Records relate to meditation. In the previous book we observed that this name is not quite an apt description. It is more valid to say that each planet develops a cultural stream. The Earth's cultural stream includes all the experiences and information that human beings have generated throughout the period they have existed on this planet. What has been called the Akaskic Records, with its suggestion of a library containing cosmic information, is better envisioned as a human-generated cultural stream that surrounds the Earth. Of course, there isn't just one stream. Each species has generated its own stream. So at the level of what, for want of a better term, is called the astral plane, multiple interlaced streams are associated with this planet. Each species' stream can be accessed by human beings. Incidentally, this is how shamans transform themselves into an eagle, snake or a jaguar. They don't enter a particular animal, rather they *drink* from the species' cultural stream. And because spiritual identities are associated with each and every species, in doing so they initiate communication with those spiritual identities.

We observe that you also generate your own personal cultural stream, which is a distillation of all your experiences, skills, knowledge and wisdom. Your personal cultural stream could be thought of as your personal Akashic Record, in which your secret multi-incarnational history is recorded. Of course, it is only hidden from your human you. Your spiritual you knows everything that is in it.

The existence of all these streams means that a vast amount of information is available to any enquiring mind. We emphasise the word *enquiring* because one of the few rules governing the acquisition of knowledge is that no one gains access to any personal or collective cultural stream without first asking. It is not that permission needs to be granted—although we note that sometimes an individual is held back from accessing information for their own good, given that the adage *a little knowledge is a dangerous thing* contains more than a germ of truth. But this is rare. What applies much more commonly is that people don't gain access to information that would certainly be useful to them because they don't seek it out in the first place. So it is not that individuals are denied access, it is that they deny themselves access. A simple request, sustained and repeated until a response is obtained, can open up much new knowledge.

Here, then, is another aspect of meditation: it involves asking for information and remaining quiet until a subtle voice presents what is sought. Most commonly, the voice you hear, the stream from which you sip, emanates from your spiritual you. After sustained practice, and in the context of what is required to fulfil your life plan, you may begin to hear other subtle voices and subsequently access alternative streams of information. The only restraints on your ability to access those streams of information are the restraints you place on yourself. No one else, no other being, is holding you back. As is written, knock and it will be opened to you. Ask and you will be answered. But no answers arrive without the questions first being asked.

What questions are best? Those that illuminate areas in your life that you wish to address. Start from who you are, where you are, doing what you are. All wisdom flows from this.

Question 3

What about meditating to find God?

Alright, I can see the point of getting insightful information about ourselves and others. But what about using meditation to find God? Mystics say they rise out of themselves and ecstatically surrender to God, YHWH, Brahman, Tao, the One, Allah, etc. Meditation as you're describing it, as a way to obtain information, doesn't appear to include this. So what's the deal with meditating to find God or using meditation to surrender to the Divine?

THE GUIDES RESPOND:

We'll begin with a question of our own. What God are you referring to? We have previously discussed the idea of God as a projection of human desires. Freud was certainly correct when he observed that human beings project God as a supernatural father who they hope will look after them during trying life conditions. Others project a supernatural mother in the form of a goddess, or of Mary, the mother of Christ.

Let's be clear. There are no supernatural gods. They are an illusion. They are ideas projected onto reality by human beings who need to feel cared for. As we have also pointed out, every single person *is* cared for. But not by God. Rather it is by close friends in spirit whose help individuals may or may not be aware arrives when needed.

Another issue rises out of this desire to be cared for by a supernatural father or mother. It is that many individuals want to surrender their life to their God's control. In doing so they are actually surrendering their responsibility to grapple with the circumstances of their own life, which involves working with purpose and effect, setting and completing challenges, and making the most of their opportunities. The religious idea that believers should surrender to God's will is self-limiting. Life is a struggle and you need to work hard to achieve anything. There is no way to sugar-coat this. The reason you took on a human body in the first place was precisely to take advantage of the circumstances life provides, to grapple and struggle and use the opportunity to evolve.

On the other hand, it is understandable that at times life becomes too much and people say, "I surrender. I'm leaving it up to you now God." Everyone has periods, even extended periods, when they feel their life circumstances are too complex or too hard. We refer particularly to when people are caught up in natural disasters, war, or economic conditions that literally squeeze the life out of them.

That at these times people surrender themselves to the mechanisms of life, to fate, or to God's will, is understandable. It may be that an individual's life plan has already incorporated the disaster and that the individual's life terminates at this point. On the other hand, everyone has friends in spirit, and these friends are always on hand to provide a hand. So remaining alert throughout even the most trying circumstances can be useful. Wars and disasters always throw up tales of miraculous survival. Sometimes such survival is entirely a matter of chance. But friends in spirit may also be involved. They intervene to ensure the trapped person survives. Why do so? Because the saved individual's life plan still has significant events to play out.

Of course, miraculous survival presupposes that the individuals didn't give up, didn't surrender themselves to immediate life circumstances. Being alert to alternative possibilities, doing what you can to stay in the game, so to speak, is a key to surviving situations that from the outside appear to be unsurvivable.

In saying this, we are not criticising those who do surrender to life circumstances. At times problematic situations become terminal, and even one's friends in spirit cannot help. What we *are* criticising is the widespread religious attitude that one's life is ultimately under the control of God and that God has formulated a fate for each person that cannot be escaped. This is incorrect. There is no such God and no such inescapable fate.

What does exist for you is your own spiritual you, your friends in spirit—some of whom are incarnated with you and some of whom are keeping an eye out from the spiritual domain—and a life plan that you yourself have selected and set in motion prior to incarnating. However, your life plan is not fixed. It exists as a template for your activities this time round, but you do not have to rigidly adhere to it. You are able to depart from it if you wish.

As we have stated elsewhere, your current life is an experiment that you have set in motion according to what you chose at the level of your spiritual self. You have anticipated certain results for this experiment, and you have particular goals that your spiritual you has set for your human you to achieve. But if something unanticipated occurs that forces a change in the plan, or even if you at the level of your human you decide to change the experiment half way though, that's fine. Your life experience changes and new life lessons come to the fore. From the perspective of spirit, it is all grist to the mill.

This brings us—finally, you might say—to the question of using meditation to find God. God in the form of a supernatural father or mother has no objective existence, being a projection of human hopes and fears. Such a God can only be found by interrogating your own fears and hopes. Once the source of those fears and hopes are understood and dissolved, the projected idea of God will dissolve too.

However, there is another notion of God that is proposed by mystics and philosophers. This is God as the ground of all existence. In Indian spirituality this ground is called Brahman, the Absolute. We would characterise this ground as unmodulated consciousness, which is beyond everything that exists physically, psychologically, mentally or spiritually. The Indian mystics proposed that atman, each individual's spiritual self, is made up of the same spiritual stuff as Brahman. This means that Brahman and atman are identical. We affirm that this is the case. You at the level of your spiritual you consist of consciousness. The ground of all existence similarly consists of consciousness. Yet though ultimately they are one, there is a difference between them. The difference is that the ground of all existence is a vast ocean of consciousness, whereas you as an individual are but a drop in it. This well-known metaphor may seem overused and somewhat simplistic, but it is as good as any other to indicate the relationship of individual consciousness to the ground of all existence. Of course, the relationship is more complex than this metaphor indicates. We'll come back to this point later.

For now we wish to make clear that how the ancient Indian mystics came to the realisation that atman and Brahman are the same stuff of consciousness was via meditation. They closed their eyes and looked within, seeking the ground of their personal being. In doing so, they discovered information about the ground of all beings. The first expositions of their discoveries were recorded in the Upanishads. This phase culminated in the *Bhagadvad Gita*, which drew together several hundred years of exploration. For another thousand years or so the sages of Vedanta and Buddhism added additional insights to what was originally perceived during meditation.

We do not disagree with their insights. If you define God as the ground of all existence, meditation will certainly enable you to access particular levels of that ground. However, and we emphasise this, there are limits on what you as an awareness currently occupying a human body are capable of perceiving. To explain the nature of these limits we need to make a digression into what are traditionally regarded as metaphysical issues—at least, incarnate human communities see them as metaphysical. For those living in discarnate spiritual communities, human or otherwise, what we are about to say is simply how reality works.

All spiritual identities—including you, us, and beings of every kind, most of which are unknown to humanity—have been manifested out of the oceanic consciousness that is ground of all existence. Each has been born, by which we mean created, by a process of spontaneous extrusion out of consciousness. Technically, each spiritual identity is a modulation of the underlying unmodulated consciousness. More simply, each is a drop of oceanic consciousness.

Not all spiritual identities function in the same way. Most remain a unified identity throughout their existence. However some, soon after their birth, splinter into smaller identities. These splinters number anywhere from just a handful to many thousands. Each spirit that incarnates into a series of human bodies is part of a much larger spiritual entity that has splintered into somewhere between eight hundred and twelve hundred separate identities. There are exceptions, with some having more and some fewer, but this is the average for those spiritual entities that choose to incarnate in the human world.

So at the level of your spiritual self you are one part of a spiritual entity that consists of between eight and twelve hundred independent separate identities. These identities form your immediate spiritual family. Most of your friends in spirit come from this family. However, as is the case within human families, you are closer to some in your spiritual family than to others. In addition, some whose company you enjoy come from other spiritual families. Naturally, you choose to incarnate more frequently with those you are closer to than with those who are not as close.

This metaphysical fact has implications for those who wish to use meditation to know God. It makes clear that several different levels of consciousness are available to the meditator. Initially, meditators lift their awareness to the level of their own spiritual self. Everyday human awareness is cramped, hemmed in and limited compared to the spiritual self's awareness, which is open, free and expansive. When you are incarnated in a human body you struggle to express your love and hard-won wisdom, but when you have no body you are much freer to emanate that love and wisdom.

When people meditate and reach this spiritual level of themselves, they are frequently overwhelmed by the intensity of what they find. As a result they think they have found and merged with God. This is not the case. They have found and merged with their own spiritual self. The contrast of what they experience, their feeling of being loved and free, reflects the contrast between normal human embodied existence and normal human non-embodied spiritual existence.

A key result of meditation is that it enables you to become aware of the fact that you participate in both levels simultaneously, that at the same time you are bodily hemmed in and spiritually free. It just takes a change in perspective to shift from one level to the other. A key truth of human existence is that human beings function on these two levels. When your body dies you will operate on just one level, the spiritual. Until then meditation helps you switch your perspective to that of your spiritual self and back again.

It is also possible to use meditation to tune in at the level of your collective spiritual family. This is an empowering, overpowering experience. Think of how intoxicating it is when your everyday awareness merges with your own spiritual self. Then multiply that by ten, by one hundred, by a thousand. As far as your human-level awareness is concerned, being united with the love and accumulated wisdom of your spiritual family would, to use the vernacular, blow you away. The experience is that intense. This is why it rarely occurs at the human embodied level. Even in a non-embodied state it takes much preparation before individual splinters are ready to merge with their full extended family. Merging on this level is an art that is learned and perfected by incarnating a thousand or more times into the human world.

There are further levels of potential merging. Each collected family of spiritual identities merges with other similar groups of collective identities in ways that cannot be described here, both because it has no meaning on the human level and because human concepts of love and surrender are inadequate to describe what is involved. So we are not being coy in withholding information, it is simply that it would be like trying to describe the principles of higher mathematics to a goldfish. Knowledge of what is involved will come when you complete your cycle of incarnations, rise of out the fishbowl that is life on this planet, and move on to encounter what comes next.

All this means there are numerous levels for your awareness to rise through before it can merge with the pure unmodulated consciousness that is the ground of all existence. Just as all spiritual identities emerged out of this ground, so all will eventually return to it. However, from a human perspective, this is a long way in the future.

In the meantime, is it possible for individuals to merge with this ground of unmodulated consciousness? After all, people have written accounts of feeling their awareness lifted into another realm, which is sometimes characterised as heaven, sometimes as a void, sometimes as shamanic worlds, sometimes as hyper-dimensional space, and having the feeling of coming into contact with the ground of consciousness. We offer two observations.

First, human beings have long been conditioned by their religions to think of spiritual reality as ultimately consisting of the human soul and God. Between the human soul and God, separating them, are heaven and hell, which are inhabited by beings such as angels and demons. So when human beings experience a spiritual presence, and they know it isn't an angel or devil, they assume they have experienced God. What they perceive is truly perceived, but their interpretation of their perception is incorrect. Traditional religious notions have led them astray.

Second, what gives rise to these erroneous notions is humanity's tendency towards being grandiose. It has long been an assumption among the religious, and more recently among those who practise the sciences, that human beings are the only conscious beings in physical existence. As a result, the idea has risen that human truths are universal truths and that as the ancient Greek philosopher asserted *man is the measure of all things*—and we deliberately retain the sexist term to reinforce just how limited such a proposition is.

The fact is that human beings, women and men, are not the measure of anything beyond their own experience. No single person is even the measure of all human experience, given how varied life is in the human world and that no one has tried every possible human activity and skill, let alone become expert in them all. In addition, human psychological make-up varies immensely, with some happily enjoying experiences that others find highly distasteful, even repellent. As another homily puts it, there is no accounting for taste. The upshot is that one person's measure, which results from their experience and judgement, is certainly not the same as someone else's measure. To place the cap on this line of thought, we observe that humanity's collective perception and judgement provides just one possible measure of reality among innumerable measures applied by all the different species living throughout the universe.

So, far from being the measure of all things, human beings struggle to provide a coherent measure even for everything that occupies them for the duration of their lives. Do not think that we are being sarcastic or sneering when we say this. We too lived many human lives during which we thought that our perceptions, along with our tastes, assumptions and judgements, provided a valid measure for all things. With experience comes wisdom, with wisdom comes humility, and humility involves the realisation that one should not speculate or make grandiose assumptions regarding matters for which one lacks the full facts.

To end this answer to the question on using meditation to merge with God, we offer the unavoidably deflating response that you should keep your focus close to home. If you are able to freely contact and merge with your spiritual self whenever you wish, and if you develop knowledge of what members of your own spiritual family are doing in relation to your life plan and what you are doing in relation to theirs, then you have achieved a great deal.

Leave God to do God's business, whatever that might be. The business of making the most of your opportunities of being human is more than sufficient to grapple with in the short time you have available to you in this life. Paradoxically, it is also the most effective way to find God. Everything that exists is a manifestation of the ground of all existence. By exploring the world we are living in right now we are engaging with the manifestations and modulations of unmanifest and unmodulated consciousness. As the old adage wisely states, we each find God by finding ourselves in the midst of whatever reality we currently inhabit.

Question 4

How come people see Jesus, Krishna and angels?

You say there's no supernatural God and that a supernatural being like Mary the mother of Christ doesn't exist. Yet people have seen her. People have seen Christ. People have seen Krishna, Ram, Kali. Then there are all the angels and demons people claim have visited them. What is really going on with perceptions of supernatural beings? Are they real?

THE GUIDES RESPOND:

It is true that the histories of all the world's religions and mystical traditions are filled with accounts of people's encounters with non-embodied beings of many kinds. As you stated, angels, demons, deceased saints, Gods and gods—we differentiate because a God that influences millions in one era can become diminished into a god that has little or no impact at a later time—have been perceived by numerous mystics, and even by ordinary believers, although when people have such perceptions they are in states that are more mystical than ordinary. The question is asked, if we state no such beings exist, and yet many people have equally firmly stated they have seen them, then what is actually occurring?

In religious traditions, if someone sees a revered individual in spirit, that person is considered to be blessed, to have undergone a miraculous experience, and so to be special to the God that tradition worships. Is this all delusion? Yes. And no. The question demands a simple response, yet once again the psychology of what is involved is complex. In fact, what occurs during such perceptions is so complex there cannot be a single answer, or group of answers, that adequately accounts for what occurs. Ideally, each situation should be addressed case by case. Clearly, we are unable to do that here. So we will make the most of this opportunity and offer some general statements that we hope will clarify at least a little of what is involved. But before doing so we need to lay a foundation on which to construct our response.

First, it must be understood that human beings are conditioned by their environment. Conditioning begins with the biological, in the sense that the majority of human beings are brought up in the belief that their identity is bound up in a body. This is true, but equally not true. It is not true because you are a spiritual identity who has chosen to inhabit a body for a period of time. Before, during and after inhabiting a body you continue to be a spiritual being who has an ongoing spiritual existence. So you are not bound into a body. Yet it is true that your identity *is* bound to a body in the sense that forgetting your spiritual identity is part of the deal when you are born human.

The way to reconcile these two apparently contradictory levels of identity is to say that the *human you* you are this time round is a sub-identity, a sub-personality, of your ongoing *spiritual you*. Your human sub-identity has been born and will die, whereas your spiritual identity continues, growing and evolving life by life, sub-personality by sub-personality, across human eons.

What is a human sub-personality? It is a psychological construct that results when your innate human traits interact with, and react against, social conditions and the personalities of those you grow up with. The way this occurs is complex. If you wish to explore all that is involved we direct you to the books *Practical Spirituality* and *Psychological Spirituality*. For our purpose here we will say that the personality of your human you contains specific talents and traits. Some you have inherited genetically, some you adopted from your parents and peers by copying them, and some you have brought into this life, having developed them in prior lives. Some of your talents and traits are positive, some are negative, some help you achieve your goals, and some work against what you want to achieve.

More simply, people can be said to contain shadow and light. No one is wholly shadow or wholly light, although some individuals certainly raditate more light and some radiate more shadow. In every life each individual has shadow issues they are dealing with. They also possess light that illuminates their existence and the lives of those they interact with. It has always been so with human existence, and will always be so.

So you as an identity have a body-focused identity and an associated personality driven by specific psychological traits. On top of both these levels of identity is placed a matrix of beliefs. Each individual views the world and interprets what it sees via this matrix. We use the word *matrix* because no one possesses a single set of beliefs. Everyone has multiple sets of beliefs laid over one another, criss-crossing to form layered patterns.

For example, beliefs about body dictate ideas of beauty and ugliness, which in turn generate admiration or distaste. A body shape that is considered attractive in one place is not so elsewhere. Skin colour has long been a factor in identity. Ideas around race, racial differences, racial superiority and inferiority, the practice of racial profiling, and judgements of whether another individual is a friend or foe, all use skin colour as a marker of identity. Biological markers have also long been used to generate social identity from which are derived notions of class and caste, higher and lower, worthy and unworthy, pure and tainted. The same points could be repeated in relation to sexual characteristics and orientation. Biased ideas grounded in biological and social identity have been sustained throughout human history and continue today.

Finally, there are the ideas people have about themselves and the world. These ideas are social, anti-social, economic, scientific, genetic, artistic, religious, metaphysical, psychological, philosophical, cosmological, neurological, numerological, biological, humanistic, linguistic, Darwinist, hubristic, war-seeking, peace-seeking ... the list goes on. Innumerable ideas are available throughout the human domain that people adopt.

For many individuals, their most cherished ideas, the ideas that they consider define them as human beings, were socially conditioned into them during childhood. This is especially the case with religious beliefs and attitudes. Key ideas are also absorbed from peers during childhood and imbibed via education, whether it be state supplied education, or religious education, or an education obtained on the sly, involving notions deliberately adopted to contradict parental decrees or social norms. Related to this are the ideas consciously adopted and worked through during the teen period and adulthood, when individuals question the attitudes and beliefs in which they were raised.

Whether ideas are unconsciously absorbed during childhood or willingly adopted in adulthood, everyone perceives the world through a matrix of ideas. Some of these ideas are matters of belief, adopted because they feel right and not because they reflect the nature of reality. Other ideas have been thoroughly tested and found to be correct. Most people's ideas fall between these two extremes. Whether tested or uncritically accepted, ideas may be true, be false, be ideas people want to be true, be ideas people suspect are false but think really what's the difference?, or be ideas people go along with because it is to their advantage or simply because living is just easier that way.

Once again we have gone on a long disquisition before we are in a position to answer the question. However, this has been necessary because we need to establish a context in which to offer a response. The context is that it is always a particular human identity that perceives anything in the world. As we have been at pains to point out, this human identity is shaped by a range of biological, social and psychological factors, and perceives the world through a matrix of beliefs. So we are now in a position to address the question: When an individual perceives a saint, angel, demon or god, what is going on? Are they actually perceiving what they think they see? Or are they really perceiving nothing at all? Alternatively, are they perceiving something, but it is actually different from what they think they see?

The fact is that, depending on the individual involved and the circumstances of their perception, each of these three responses can apply. Sometimes people do perceive what they think they are seeing. Sometimes nothing is there. And sometimes they are projecting their own assumptions, hopes and fears onto an actually existing spiritual identity, seeing a god where there is only a presence, or perceiving a threat where actually friendly communication is intended. Much more rarely, they may be welcoming as friendly an identity they would be better off leaving alone. These latter responses come broadly under the category of projection and interpretation.

People project and interpret according to their assumed beliefs. Because standard human notions of identity are body-bound, when people think they see a spiritual being they see a particular bodily form because that is what they have been taught to expect. This kind of expectation applies when people see the Virgin Mary, Krishna, Christ or a saint. They perceive an actual spiritual presence, then project onto it the body image they have been conditioned to expect. In this case, a spiritual presence is perceived in a particular humanised form due to projected interpretation. All this assumes that spiritual identities really do exist to be perceived. This is certainly the case.

However, a second category of actual perception applies, because it is not just perceivers' projections that lead to spiritual identities being seen as Krishna, Christ, Buddha, Kali, the Virgin Mary, or in the form of a saint. On occasion, a spiritual identity may deliberately adopt the guise of Krishna, Christ and so on. Why do so? Is trickery involved? Once again, yes and no. Yes, trickery is involved because in reality the spiritual identity does not exist in the form the perceiver sees. On the other hand, genuine communication does take place, motivated by a loving intent. The identity adopts that particular guise so the person may be comforted by a form they recognise. Familiarity reduces the fear that naturally rises in human beings when they meet something outside what is normal. This familiar form makes them more open to receiving what is being communicated. It may be an answer to a question, it may be guidance relative to a crucial life decision, or it may be to provide a boost at a time when the individual is feeling depressed or deflated. We repeat, a spiritual identity may adopt a familiar form in order to break down the barriers that normally exist between the spiritual and human domains.

A third category of perceptions occurs in the context of the cultural streams we mentioned earlier. Each religious and spiritual tradition has its own cultural stream containing characteristic rituals, formulas, imagery, metaphors, concepts and texts. Each stream also has individuals who have made a significant contribution during that tradition's history. All this is useful to spiritual identities as they strive to communicate with human beings who are working within a particular tradition and whose beliefs are defined by it. In effect, the cultural stream provides a language and ready-made symbols and concepts to facilitate communication. Enquiring believers who are given insights by helpful spiritual identities receive them via familiar religious symbols, through symbolic dreams, and via visions in which a significant historical figure is perceived. Those who have these kinds of perceptions are often so impressed by them that they conclude their tradition's symbols and historical figures are deep truths. For the spiritual identity who provides the insights, the same religious symbols and figures are merely artefacts of that tradition's cultural stream, conveniently at hand to facilitate communication.

Everyone needs language to talk to another. Cultural streams provide the required language. However, cultural streams have a downside. Over time, baggage builds up within each stream. When those who receive insights from the spiritual domain use their cultural stream to interpret their experiences, their interpretation is tainted by baggage. As a result they alter what is communicated to them, sometimes to a great degree. So while on the one hand the artefacts present within cultural streams can facilitate communication due to both sides sharing an understanding of what those ideas, symbols and metaphors mean, on the other hand cultural baggage can lead to the misinterpretation of what has been communicated.

By *baggage* we refer to various human-created ideas regarding what the spiritual domain consists of, how people should think and behave in the human domain, and how the two domains are related. As a religious tradition ages, it accumulates more and more baggage, which believers adopt. This makes the tradition's cultural stream less and less effective for sustaining direct and unadulterated communication between the spiritual and human domains.

To conclude, spiritual identities exist and are perceived, but human beings have a tendency either to accept such perceptions at face value, or to reject them as unlikely or impossible. The current clashes in public forums between believers and unbelievers, between the curious and the sceptical, as well as the conflicts that occur within individuals as they struggle to process perceptions outside the range of what is normal, reflect the extent to which confusion exists around perceptions of spiritual identities. This is because there is little acknowledgement of the degree to which individuals affect what they perceive. We repeat, all debates about whether or not spiritual identities exist externally to the observing individual, and regarding the true nature of such identities, need to recognise the degree to which such perceptions are impacted by internal processing.

How can I know
who I'm talking to?

Actually, I'm not sure how comforting that last answer is. You say spiritual identities really do communicate with us, but our inner processing affects our reception of what they say. If that's so, how can I know who I'm talking to—assuming I really am talking to someone else and not just muttering inanities to myself?

THE GUIDES RESPOND:

This question is common to everyone when they begin communicating with the spiritual realm that exists beyond the realm of physical human experience—although, to be accurate, the spiritual doesn't really exist beyond the physical realm. It is more accurate to say the spiritual realm exists in parallel to human reality, right beside it.

When individuals first attempt to shift their awareness, which is dominated by the experience of physical reality, and seek to communicate with the spiritual realm—when, using the terms we introduced earlier, they begin shifting their focus from their human you to their spiritual you—doubts arise. This is natural. It is natural because seekers are making their first tentative steps into new territory, and trepidation, uncertainty, even fear, naturally accompany such steps. So lack of clarity as to whether communications are spiritual or merely imagined arises because the communications are subtle. In contrast, the emotions of trepidation, uncertainly and fear are powerful. That you are entering new territory ensures doubt is inevitable. So the question is itself not only natural, it is unavoidable.

We liken this situation to a child's first day at school, or to an adult's first day at a new job, when the environment is unfamiliar and you fear that what is expected of you is beyond your capabilities. Clearly, you are out of your comfort zone. Yet you are also excited because of the possibilities this new environment offers. At least, we hope excitement outweighs the trepidation and fear!

This is how we view the context in which this question is being asked. It's an excellent question, because the fact you're asking it means you are being challenged. New perceptions are pushing you out of what you know and have become comfortable with, out of the established patterns established by your gloopy self and into unexplored regions of your self, which is where the subtle signals are being received. No matter that you are uncertain of the source of the signals, the fact you are receiving signals at all is to be celebrated.

This, then, is our first answer to the question: be happy that you are uncertain. It is a significant step towards becoming spiritually knowing. Note that we say it is a *significant* step and not a *first* step, because it is not a first step. Anyone for whom this question is important has done a great deal of prior work to reach this stage in their development.

We add that continuing to question perceptions, no matter how experienced you may be in receiving signals that come from beyond your human you, is a trait we encourage. We encourage it because—and we are now commenting on the development of spiritual insight—people are like frogs. That is, people tend to progress by jumps rather than smoothly, one step at a time. We'll explain.

Imagine a frog is sitting on a large leaf floating in a pond. The leaf symbolises the familiar everyday world. The frog is comfortable sitting there. However, a time comes when the frog gets tired of its familiar world. It wants to extend itself, to experience something new. So what does it do? It jumps. Perhaps it jumps onto a new leaf in the pond, changing its perspective, so the world now appears slightly different to how it did. Or perhaps the frog jumps out of the pond altogether, into a new pond. Wherever it lands, a settling-in period follows, after which the new place likely becomes as familiar and comfortable as the previous one.

This is what people do both spiritually and in their everyday lives. They become dissatisfied with their experiential inputs. Eventually, the dissatisfaction becomes so intense that they feel compelled to make a jump. They then land in a new place, which leads to a new view of the world. Perhaps it provides a different way of relating, or initiates a different way of behaving, or offers a different way of living. In using the word *different* we are assuming it incorporates a feeling of greater satisfaction than such individuals previously experienced. After a settling-in period, this different, more satisfying situation becomes their new normal. However, what people rarely do is start questioning the new place in which they have landed. Satisfied that life has changed, they don't ask themselves if this is where they can satisfy *all* the levels of their self—because the reality is that more new perspectives, new information, new feelings, new knowledge and new relationships are available to them. Much more exists to be explored. However, it will only become available if it is actively sought.

Accordingly, we recommend that you don't think of yourself as a frog. Don't think that spiritual development involves a single leap or that it incorporates one fundamental change. Instead, think of yourself as a mountaineer or a long distance runner, that your spiritual quest involves a challenging climb or a long journey. Certainly, pause long enough to acknowledge the ways that each place, feeling or item of knowledge you experience is satisfying and meaningful to you. Then acknowledge that this is not a destination to settle into permanently, it is merely a step towards what comes next.

Of course, if you adopt this advice you will never be quite settled, never be completely certain, never be fully fulfilled. But we suggest that this is a good thing, because it will result in your horizon continuously opening out. You won't have the mindset that your happiness merely depends on finding a better pond with a change in food and a larger leaf to sit on. Your mindset will be that each place you arrive at is a valuable staging post on your journey towards the ocean.

This realisation provides another context in which to consider the question, because there is always something more, existing beyond the current limits of your perception, that once you become aware of it will destabilise what you know. Ordinary life involves establishing a stable balance between you, the people you regularly interact with, and the familiar world you all share. In contrast, a spiritual journey is one of imbalance, in the sense that it forces you to re-evaluate the familiar relationships that stabilise your everyday existence.

Be aware that we are equating stability with being static. We introduce the word *static* here because it illuminates an important facet of what is required in order to progress spiritually. A normal life is stable, in the sense that the individual has established a relationship between the physical and spiritual realms, a relationship that is static.

The way each individual relates the physical to the spiritual is usually set in place by late childhood. Essentially, it involves the individual accommodating the physical to the spiritual in a way that feels comfortable. This accommodation applies whether the individual acknowledges the spiritual realm or ignores it completely. By late childhood the accommodation is crystallised into a set attitude. Because it is crystallised, individuals become static. They are not going anywhere—of course, we mean this in a spiritual sense, that their understanding of the relationship between the physical and the spiritual is no longer developing.

Now consider what is involved in *not* being static. Imagine what is required to keep moving. To do so, think of what it takes to walk.

Walking requires that you lift one foot and move it forwards. This creates a posture of imbalance. If you didn't compensate for the imbalance you would fall over. But you do compensate by shifting your weight from the grounded leg to the leg which is outstretched. As a result of shifting your weight you take a step forwards. You could then draw up your following leg, place it beside your grounded leg, and take up a static posture once again. Or you could keep your following leg moving through, shift your weight onto it, lift your newly following leg, and repeat the process. In this way you walk. So it can be said that walking requires a continuous state of imbalance.

We offer this as an analogy, to show you how a state of never being settled, of never being in balance, results in forward movement. Imbalance leads to progress. More significantly, imbalance is *absolutely necessary* to progress. So rather than maintaining the traditional religious and spiritual pairs of good and bad, of ignorance and wisdom, we suggest you adopt the conceptual pairs of balance and imbalance, stasis and progression. To reiterate, when you feel off-balance, when you are uncertain where your foot will land next, such a state is spiritually advantageous.

We now come back to the question of how someone who seeks to establish a newly adjusted relationship with the spiritual realm may identify the sources of communications apparently emanating from that realm, and may also be certain that such communications aren't imagined, that they don't merely involve you talking to yourself.

We'll start with the second part of this question, the issue of whether a subtle stream of thought is imagined. Our response begins by asking: within you, what is the source of imagined communications? The answer is there is only one source of imagined communications. It is your gloopy self. The gloopy self is built on a bedrock of fear. Fear of the unknown, fear of the new, fear of threats, and fear of whatever is destabilising, is what led to your gloopy self growing inside you in the first place. The gloopy self then projects its feelings onto the world. Sometimes these feelings are justified, usually they are not. And even when there is some justification for their coming into existence, such as when there really is a threat, the gloopy self extends its response far beyond what is actually required to deal effectively with the situation. These projected feelings are imagination in action.

Elsewhere we have called the gloopy self a psychological compensating mechanism. It forms patterns of processing and behaviour within the human psyche to help individuals cope with the vicissitudes of life. Because vicissitudes occur from birth, and for many people even before birth (due to emotional and physiological stress affecting both mother and fetus during pregnancy), your gloopy self's patterns of compensating behaviour are deeply ingrained in your psyche. We have previously likened the gloopy self to a pole that, by adulthood, stands solidly in place, its base buried deep in compensating attitudes, behaviours and fears that go back to childhood. During their life people cling to their pole, making it the centre of what they do to cope whenever the winds of vicissitudes blow. Because everyone clings to their own individual pole—that is, because everyone accommodates themselves to the behaviour, feelings and thoughts emanating from their gloopy self—their gloopy self becomes the static centre around which their sense of identity forms.

Accordingly, when you are trying to decide whether unusual, subtle communications are real or imagined, two possibilities arise. Both involve your gloopy self. One is that they are entirely imagined, and your gloopy self is the source. The other is that the subtle communications are not imagined, but your gloopy self fears being destabilised by them and so generates doubt, trepidation, and uncertainty regarding them. Indeed, whenever you receive feelings or ideas that are not usual for you, you can expect doubts and fears to follow. Know that the gloopy self is the source of those doubts and fears.

This being the case, your question becomes: How should I proceed when a subtle impression arrives, whether during meditation, in dreams, during quiet moments, or when you are engaged in an everyday activity and a thought unexpectedly pops into your awareness that is different to normal?

Our advice is, firstly, take it seriously. Treat it as important. Don't shrug it off, brush it away, or assume it is imagined. If you don't take it seriously you'll never find out if it is potentially useful. In fact, even if you initially think it *is* imagined, still treat it seriously. You can decide later whether it is or isn't.

Second, record it, so you don't forget it. There are plenty of life distractions, which are unhelpful, because getting caught up in them leads you to forget the subtle impressions that occasionally enter your awareness. Drawing your attention away from subtle impressions towards distractions is another strategy the gloopy self uses to sustain its stasis.

Third, with your impressions on record, you are in a position to weigh their validity. Validation is essential. Much could be said about this. Briefly, validation is a process by which you seek other impressions, other experiences, which confirm a previous impression or experience. Often this involves a waiting game, because it may be days, weeks or even years before you receive what you consider to be sufficiently strong confirmation to validate your original impression and show it wasn't imagined. This is a further reason why keeping records is useful: you can look back to when you had a similar perception, no matter how long ago that was, and contrast and compare it to what you have recently perceived. Of course, some impressions are so distinctive and vivid that they remain with you for the rest of your life.

Fourth, once you find that the subtle communication is not imagined, that it is one of a number of similar communications that come from outside the thoughts and feelings that are a normal part of your psyche, you have validation. Of course, what you do with the validated communication, whether you reject it or respond to it, and *how* you respond to it, is another issue again. We'll deal with it another time.

We stress that taking a subtle communication seriously is at the heart of our response to the question. If you take it seriously enough to record it, it then remains available to you to come back to and ponder. By weighing it up at a quiet time when you have the time, focus and energy to do so, you are in a position to eventually validate the communication as real and valuable or reject it because it is not. But if you don't take the communication seriously in the first place, if you shrug it off as merely being one of those strange things that occur in life, you are allowing your gloopy self to dominate your response. Your gloopy self doesn't want challenging, unsettling, unbalancing communications. It wants stasis. Doubt is a manifestation of the defense mechanisms it uses to sustain stasis, to keep the frog sitting on the same leaf, looking at the same view, experiencing the same inputs, until it dies.

We offer one final observation about doubt and seriousness. You can experience them both at once. You can take a subtle communication seriously enough to write it down, yet at the same time doubt it means anything at all. Doubt and seriousness can be present together because doubt emanates from your gloopy self and seriousness from your higher self. The two levels exist side by side within you, and your awareness is perfectly capable of listening to both at the same time.

In fact, a definition of being spiritual is that both levels feed an individual's awareness and decision-making. Your human you and your spiritual you can and do operate simultaneously. Spiritual progress involves bringing your human you and your spiritual you into alignment and having them walk together, hand in hand. The more you bring these two facets of yourself into coordination, the more you develop an appreciation of things spiritual.

Question 6

How can I tune into subtle communications?

So you're saying tuning into subtle communications requires us to be in a state of permanent imbalance. But who wants to always be uncomfortable? It's a recipe for psychological disaster. To answer my own question, I guess you're suggesting we need to replace everyday stasis with spiritual openness. But how do we do that? How do we even tune in in the first place?

THE GUIDES RESPOND:

We're not suggesting you abandon your current life and commitments. Let's clear that up right away. To explain what we mean we need to introduce a new idea here, that each person lives in an inner world and an outer world. Consequently, you have an inner life and an outer life.

It will immediately be clear to those who have closely followed our previous answers that the king of your inner world is your spiritual you, while the king of your outer world is your human you. We deliberately use the antiquated term *king* because it sheds light on an important aspect of how your inner and outer worlds are ruled. In ancient times a king had a chief minister, a vizier, who advised him on decisions. Similarly, you have your own principal advisor. In fact, two. The chief minister who advises your spiritual self is the store of wisdom you have accumulated over multiple lifetimes, while the chief minister for your human you is your gloopy self.

The way these advisors function differs significantly. In your inner world, the wisdom you have accumulated during all your prior lives exists as a store that contains experiences and life lessons you can draw on when you need guidance. This especially happens between lives, when you are considering what situations you should select for your next incarnation and what will best provide the lessons you need to develop both your human you and your spiritual you. Advice on what to select is also offered by mentors, much as an ancient king had secondary ministers who filled out what the vizier didn't know. However, all the decisions on what you do in your next life ultimately remain in your hands, at the level of your spiritual you. It is for this reason that we say your spiritual you is king of your inner world.

The situation with your human you is quite different. As we are all well aware, human existence is an arena of contesting demands. Where, between lives, your spiritual you exists in a calm, supportive environment, your human you is buffeted on all sides by competing forces. It is attacked, has to defend itself, is cut, and makes cuts of its own. Some of these cuts are deliberate, many are accidental. As a result, human existence is full of impinging situations that demand a response. When your human you is on top of those demands—which most commonly occurs in adulthood after you have worked your way into a life situation where the daily cut and thrust remains at a level you can cope with—then you achieve a state of relative happiness and contentment. But when the demands are more than you can cope with, your life becomes chaotic and unhappiness reigns.

Of course, your spiritual you initiated its descent into this demanding human situation in the first place. It did so in order to learn. But as the complexities of human life multiply, and as the demands of everyday existence require more and more of your attention, the voice of your spiritual you becomes lost in all the noise and ends up buried deep inside you. As a result, the store of wisdom your spiritual you has to draw on, wisdom that is there to bolster you and guide you during tough times, becomes not just inaudible among everything else shouting at you, it effectively becomes inaccessible.

In this situation, the one voice that is able to cut through the clatter is the voice of your gloopy self. It can do so because this is its world. As we pointed out earlier, the gloopy self is a psychological coping mechanism that starts forming in childhood precisely to help you deal with the vicissitudes of life. It grows in the human world of cut and counter-thrust. It learns how to duck and dive, deny and equivocate. The bread and butter of its existence involves pretending. It lies while seeming to tell the truth, stares down attacks, and runs away or attacks when all else fails. As a consequence of having to cope with tricky life experiences, the gloopy self has learned what side its bread is buttered on. It knows how and when to butter up others, when to barter its butter for personal advantage, and when it is best to simply surrender its butter to others.

Of course, the gloopy self is only one aspect of your human you. Your human you has multiple layers. There is your body and its genetically inherited physical traits. You also have genetically inherited emotional and intellectual traits, embodied in your limbic and cognitive systems, which provide innate abilities along with innate weaknesses—potential weaknesses include a genetic disposition to suffer from certain diseases and a psychological potential to experience certain forms of psychosis. You also have what could be termed a learning self, the part of you that learns skills, as well as a creative self that adapts those skills to your own delight. You have a thinking self that tries to make sense of life situations and experiences, which may grow through talking and reading, or be overtaken by dogma or by others' revelatory, dumb or destructive ideas. All these layers, and much else, contribute to your human you. So your gloopy self is only one among many competing presences that shape your current human you.

The problem is that where your store of wisdom awaits your spiritual you's enquiry, and so maintains a passive relationship to you, your gloopy self actively dominates your human you. In part this is a necessity, because you have to socially interact with others and it provides a set of attitudes and behaviours that facilitate interaction. Where your gloopy self is detrimental to you is that it has grown out of a fear-based relationship to the world. Basically, it is a psychological defense mechanism. It also wants stability, because that is a safer state for it than imbalance. So the gloopy self's natural propensity is towards stasis. As such, it inhibits growth. Because it naturally dominates your psyche and your interactions with others, in order to grow you need to diminish the gloopy self's dominance within you. The only way to do that is by engaging in psychological self-transformative work. There are many ways to carry out this task. We have made recommendations in the *Channelled Spirituality* series of books. Numerous other effective sets of advice are also available. You just need to seek them out.

To recap then, for individuals who have not worked on themselves psychologically, their inner world is naturally dominated by their stasis-promoting gloopy self, and the subtle voice of their spiritual self is buried deep beneath the clatter generated during the course of daily living. For those who wish to become sensitive to subtle communications, the relationship existing in your inner world—in which the active gloopy self dominates the quiet spiritual self—has to be changed. Psychologically, you need to reverse the relationship and make your gloopy self passive and your spiritual active. To do this, you need to eradicate many of the gloopy self's traits and replace the fear at its foundations with positive qualities. This is, literally, the work of a lifetime.

In practice, the change in inner relationship occurs incrementally. The good news is that at any time you can create an inner clearing within your psyche, where your human you's awareness can set up camp for a period of time free of the everyday clatter and free of the daily demands that spark the gloopy self into defensive action. In effect, meditation situates you in a low stimulus environment. Deliberately mentally disengaging from the outer world allows you, in your inner world, to direct your attention towards your spiritual you and hear what it has to say. When you wish to address life problems or gather information on a particular topic, your spiritual you can draw on its store of wisdom and communicate it to you. So, very straightforwardly, meditation provides a means for you to start changing the way your inner world functions. It enables your spiritual you to actively provide input into your daily existence. And it helps you create a new balance between your spiritual self and your human self. Of course, working on your psychology will speed up this rebalancing a hundred-fold.

At this point we wish to comment on an insufficiently discussed aspect of the inner and outer worlds. Each contains many levels. In your outer world, the first level you have is the immediate environment in which your body moves. It is filled with your tribe, which consists of family, friends, work colleagues and all those you interact with regularly. This portion of the outer world dominates your attention. It is from there that the most urgent demands in your life originate. However, this immediate level is itself dominated by much larger social, economic and cultural forces. This second level of the outer world provides the rules you and those you immediately interact with live by. It is communal and national in nature. It dictates how relationships may occur and how people may live. Beyond this is a third level. It is international and intercultural. In the past this level had very little direct impact on people's lives, but today, with the internet, the activities of multinational corporations, and easy access to international travel, the third level has a major impact on everyone's lives. With linked banking systems, the ability to shift economic activity quickly from one country to another, and the drive to generate profits without regard to the cost to others, this third level commonly over-rides second level communal and national forces and agreements, to the discomfort of many. The fourth level is that of the planet, within which the first three levels exist. Certain fundamental inputs into your existence come from this level, such as gravity, the air you breath, and the biological processes that have evolved within the biosphere that provide you with a body and its nutrition. So, these four levels provide the environment for your wider immediate existence.

We use the phrase *wider immediate existence* because the planet, in turn, exists within the solar system, which constitutes the fifth level, the solar system has its place in the local community of solar systems in this region of the Milky Way galaxy, which is the sixth level. The seventh level consists of the galaxy itself. Human beings know very little about the forces and identities that exist on these outer levels and have an input into your existence.

We could keep expanding outwards, noting that the Milky Way is part of what is called the local group of galaxies, that the local group is part of a wider group, and so on. There are many, many more levels to the outer world. But given humanity is currently limited to living on this planet and is only able to use mechanical devices to observe and listen to a narrow range of the innumerable frequencies that ripple through the universe, there is no need to list them further. It is enough to make the point that your existence in the outer world is sustained and shaped by a vast series of levels. Moreover, these levels are not just physical: They involve practical, emotional, intellectual, social, cultural, economic, and intentional decision-making—because human beings are far from the only conscious beings existing in the universe.

To turn now to your inner world, its first level consists of the bodily level attention that all animals possess and utilise to survive. As you are a human being, your animal attention is augmented by your brain's neocortex and its limbic and cognitive systems, which enable you to make complex observations of the world around you and to respond in equally complex ways. Beyond this first level is that of your socialised self, which is shaped by upbringing and cultural inputs. As we noted earlier, in those who have not worked to counteract its influence, this level is dominated by the gloopy self. The third level involves higher human activities, which are practical, emotional and intellectual in nature. They are intended and creative. We are referring here to such activities as horticulture, animal breeding, architecture, astrophysics, religion and the arts. They exist beyond the animal level, given none are required to ensure the human species' biological survival. The next inner level is energetic. It encompasses what is known as the aura, plus other kinds of subtle energy that facilitate communications between awareness at the physical and spiritual levels. The fifth level is the spiritual self.

These five levels provide the immediate inputs into your inner as a embodied human being. It can be seen that functioning at the third level—of the higher human capacities—with any kind of sophistication is beyond the capacities of most of the world's population. This is why individuals reincarnate so many times. Learning how to function effectively as a spiritual consciousness inside a human body, using all that body's physical, emotional and cognitive capacities, is a complex and very difficult task. The task involves the requirement to develop an inner psychological balance that manifests in socially considerate behaviour. This includes learning how to navigate through challenging social situations and to act considerately towards all creatures on the planet. Added to all this is the need to develop higher human capacities that are creative and contribute to the betterment of all, learning how to perceive and manipulate the aura and other subtle energies, and, the cap on everything, establishing your spiritual self as the king of your inner world. It takes multiple lifetimes to learn how to do all this.

Beyond these five inner levels are others. The sixth level is your multi-incarnational self, which contains all the personalities you have developed during all your incarnations. Then there is the larger spiritual entity of which you are a fragment. And the even larger entity of which it, in turn, forms a part. At each of these levels more spiritual environments become accessible. Just as the physical universe is vast and contains uncountable galaxies, each containing startlingly diverse worlds, so the spiritual realm contains uncountable levels and regions and is filled with an unimaginably diverse range of identities. As you evolve, and so become an increasingly wise fragment of an evolving spiritual entity, these realms and identities will become available to you—assuming, of course, you wish to engage with them.

What we are attempting to do here is indicate the extensiveness of the outer and inner worlds in which you exist. The fact you are largely unaware of them in no way diminishes their impact on your life. Initiating spiritual development involves starting to become aware of them. You can only do this progressively. Accordingly, we recommend you pay attention to the four levels of the outer world that constitute life on this planet, and to the biological, social, higher human, energetic and spiritual levels that constitute your inner world.

A final significant aspect of your inner and outer worlds to which we draw your attention here is that they do not exist separate from one another. There is no great divide that has severed your inner world from your outer world. They are a continuum. We commented earlier that prior to incarnation you, at the level of your spiritual you, selected the major situations and relationships you are occupied by during this life. This preselection process included selecting a particular body along with its genetically defined capacities, selecting a family and social environment to be born into, and deciding what higher human capacities you would seek to develop this time round. So the immediate outer world in which you currently live is not accidental. It has been chosen by you. As a result, it offers favourable circumstances for your continued growth as a spirit occupying a human body. In this way, your outer world reflects the intent of your inner self. Your outer life provides what you need to grow your inner life. This especially applies to the key relationships, the key activities, and the key choices that drive your life. Your outer world reflects the needs of your inner self.

The question has been asked, how do you tune into the subtle communications that whisper within your inner world? Meditation is certainly effective on a day-to-day basis. It helps you create a quiet space within, as it holds the everyday clatter at bay. This adds to the conditions required for subtle communications to be heard. However, the question uses the term *tuning in*. This term implies that, just as a radio tunes into one station at a time, so there is just one level for you to tune into inwardly. This isn't the case. As we have just explained, multiple levels function within you, so more than one spiritual level is available to you. As a result, the term *tuning in* doesn't quite capture the process involved. We'll explain.

Your overriding task is to evolve spiritually. This includes making full use of all your personal inner and outer levels. Doing so isn't so much a matter of tuning in as requiring what may more appropriately be called realignment. Human awareness is naturally caught up in the first levels of the outer world's demanding physical and social activities. Inwardly, it is dominated by biological urges and socialised psychological behaviours. All these activities are skin deep. Spiritually, what is required is for each individual to become aware of what is occurring in the outer world at the physical and social, cultural and national, international and planetary levels. At the same time each individual's awareness also needs to expand inwardly, so it encompasses the bodily, socialised, higher human, energetic and spiritual levels.

This involves a multi-faceted realignment of your sensibility. Again we emphasise, achieving realignment is a multi-life assignment. Each life involves putting one small piece into place. Eventually, a realigned human you will come into existence, a you that is entirely your creation. This is the permanent you that will not only blossom in this human realm, but that will contribute to the evolution of the greater spiritual identity of which you are a vital part.

Question 7

What form of meditation
do you recommend?

You're saying meditation will help open us to subtle communications. So do you recommend any specific form of mediation? Is there a beginner's form and an advanced form? Or should we just go with whatever works?

THE GUIDES RESPOND:

The particular form of meditation is unimportant. Some people sit, others stand, walk, sing, or sway rhythmically; different cultures and traditions have different practices. What is important is that the meditator attains a focused inner state in which the external world is shut out and the mind is directed to pay attention to subtle communications. That such a state is attained and sustained is what matters. How such a state is achieved does not matter.

This is the short answer to your question. However, there is a longer answer, which has to do with the underlying characteristics meditators need to be successful long-term. We call these characteristics attitudes of mind. They will help you establish a successful meditation practice.

Every skill in the human world requires repeated practice if it is to be performed successfully—by which we mean with a high level of competence. This applies to meditation, as it is a skill. Accordingly, the first attitude the successful meditator needs is commitment. It is only through repeated effort carried out over an extended period of time, and we are talking years here, that a high level of competence will be achieved. Certainly, small efforts will enhance health and relieve stress, as with the practice of mindfulness that is currently popular in some circles. But if you wish to engage in subtle communications with those in the spiritual domain, a sustained commitment to developing your meditation skills is required.

The next attitude involves fostering sensitivity. If you intend to become open to subtle communications, you need to increase your sensitivity to them. It might be argued that some people are naturally more sensitive, as is seen with psychics who easily connect with those in spirit, glean information about upcoming events, or know when things around them are going awry. While it is true that these people are naturally sensitive, that is only because they worked to develop their skills in previous lives. Everyone who is better than average in anything is merely expressing a skill they learned previously, whether it involves athletics, music, horticulture, engineering and so on.

So sensitivity is a learned skill. Like everything else in the human domain, developing sensitivity is both a simple and a complex task. It is simple in the sense that you just have to open yourself up and invite communication. But a state of openness is itself very difficult to achieve then sustain. All kinds of fears and doubts naturally creep in, which close down your efforts. This makes developing sensitivity a complex psychological task.

The chief blockage to becoming sensitive is self-defensiveness. Elsewhere we have described at length how fear is the principle force behind self-defensiveness. Fear of the unknown, fear of being hurt, fear of losing the way, fear of not doing what's right, fear of what will happen if you disobey your elders and betters—these are examples of the many ways fear manifests.

Doubts are another significant cause of blockage. Doubts may be quite irrational, especially when fears drive them, such as a fear of ghosts when one has never actually encountered a ghost. Alternatively, doubts may manifest in the guise of rational thoughts, taking the form of logical questions or observations: "I don't believe this is possible." "This is too weird to be true." "This communication defies common sense." "These kinds of things just don't happen." In fact, all doubts are just subtle forms of fear, because a specific fear always underlies a doubt. A useful exercise is to adopt a detached inner perspective and examine your doubts as if they belong to someone else. This will enable you to identify the fear behind the doubts you have in relation to any life situation, not just towards meditation.

To recap: In order to become open to subtle communications, meditators need to work against self-defensiveness. To achieve this, fears and doubts need to be banished, whether they take the form of irrational obstacles that stop you accepting subtle communications or of rationalising thought processes used to think them away. Understandably, this is a difficult task. In effect, it means that in order to come face to face with communications emanating from the spiritual domain you first have to come face to face with your self.

A saying common in spiritual circles is that the aspirant has to confront the dweller on the threshold. The threshold denotes the doorway that leads into the deeper reaches of your mind. The dweller stands in the doorway and prevents your entry. Psychologically, what stops you from entering is fear, doubt and over-rationalising. So the dweller on the threshold represents your own negatively impacting, self-limiting psychological traits.

We have previously named this dweller on the threshold your gloopy self. It is the monster that protects the hidden treasure sought by pirates, the dragon that must be slain in order to rescue the princess, the minotaur that keeps explorers from the centre of the labyrinth. The gloopy self, however you describe it, is what stops you stepping over the threshold. It must be slain. Of course, we are talking metaphorically, not literally. Just as you wouldn't cut off your arm just because it hurts, but would rather seek to heal what ails it and restore it to health, so you don't need to totally destroy the dweller on the threshold. You just need to transform it from an agent of self-defensiveness to an agent of inner progress. This involves transforming all negative traits into positive traits. Then the gloopy self dissolves away, the shadow that dominates your inner threshold vanishes, and you can gain access to the treasure within, which is your spiritual self.

As we have repeatedly said, dissolving the gloopy self is a long-term project. Right now, what you need to do is be able to step around the gloopy self to cross the threshold and enter your inner world. When for a short period you disengage from everyday life, you also disengage your mind from your gloopy self's preoccupations. This state of disengagement frees your mind to step across the threshold.

Yet even when the gloopy self has temporarily fallen away, and so is no longer in your way, taking that first step and listening for what is quietly calling you from what appears to be far away, can itself be a highly unsettling sensation. We are aware of many people who have sought out subtle communications, but as the communication occurred they pulled back and retreated to a safe and familiar place. What they lack is trust.

Trust is a very useful psychological tool. It helps you develop the confidence you need to step over the threshold and enter what, from the perspective of your everyday identity, is the unknown. Naturally, like every tool, trust is double-edged. Going through life naively trusting others is not recommended. The world is full of people who readily exploit those who are wide-eyed, eager and too easily surrender what they have, whether that be material goods or their desire for happiness, peace or love. Be clear that we are not talking about this kind of naive trust. Rather, we are referring to trusting yourself. Often, when people receive a subtle communication they doubt that they have received anything at all. They rationalise the communication as being imagined or as being a projection of their own desires. And even if they do accept that something of value has been communicated, they don't trust themselves to do anything with it. The traits that promote lack of self trust again manifest from the gloopy self. Overcoming these traits is actually straight-forward. It is simply a matter of training.

In some cultures, and especially within knowing families, children are taught to trust subtle communications. However, for most children today training is in the opposite direction, towards rejection of the inwardly subtle. So all that is required is for you to retrain yourself—and we acknowledge how easy it is for us to say this and how difficult it is for you to carry it out. There are two principle ways to retrain. One is in a group context, the other is solo. Which approach will work best for you is for you to discover.

Group situations, such as a meditation group in which participants openly discuss their subtle perceptions, is in general best for beginners. Being around others who can affirm that what you perceive is also being perceived by them is reassuring. It teaches you that what you are encountering might be strange, but it is certainly not uncommon. It is usual for people not to trust themselves because they lack a context in which to place their perceptions. Feeling isolated feeds uncertainty. So having others around you who are also exploring subtle perceptions provides a wider experiential context and bolsters self-confidence. This in turn builds self-trust: trust in your perceptions, that they are actually occurring, and trust that they are valid and useful. Group meditation practice facilitates the growth of self-trust. Once you have developed trust in the validity of your perceptions in a variety of situations, flying solo, so to speak, becomes easier.

We add that group meditation has another advantage over solo practice, because people meditating together generate a group energy. This energy can provide a power boost that enables not just the group as a whole to perceive more subtly than is normal, but for individuals within the group to travel further and deeper into spiritual domains than they would if they were meditating alone.

A meditation group need not be large. Three people are a group. In the Christian gospels Jesus is reported as saying that whenever two or three are gathered in his name, he will be there. Each individual has an inner Christ. Your intent to engage in subtle communications is the knock on the door. Being in a state of inner quiet enables you to open the door. You then need to step past the dweller on the threshold and enter your inner world—which is an entrance into the extensive spiritual realm. We note that instead of the word *Christ* you could equally use the terms atman, soul, Buddha nature or higher self. Each spiritual tradition has its own way of describing the same process.

To summarise, successful meditation requires you to commit to long-term practice, cultivate sensitivity, overcome the triad of self-defensiveness, fears and doubts, and learn to trust your own perceptions. To these we add a final quality, introduced in the previous response, of not being satisfied with your current levels of knowledge. A quest attitude is spiritually beneficial, of always striving to open up new trails and seeking to know more.

To conclude, we observe that while these six attitudes of mind—commitment, sensitivity, not being self-defensive, overcoming fears and doubts, learning to trust, and sustaining a quest attitude—will foster the growth of your inner life, they will equally stand you in good stead when you have to deal with the difficult situations and relationships that arise in your outer world. We invite you to ponder on how this is so for yourself.

Question 8

Stop right there! Can evil spirits threaten my life?

You say we need to learn to trust. But what about all the creepy stuff involving evil spirits? What about succubi like the demon Lilith, who feeds off sexual energy, and demons that possess people and drive them mad? What about them? Should I be scared? Can evil spirits really threaten my life?

THE GUIDES RESPOND:

There is a great deal of misinformation, including wilfully embroidered stories, regarding the existence and nature of so-called evil spirits. We can't deal with all that is claimed in a short response such as this, but we can illuminate some of what is involved. We'll begin by offering a story that provides a useful metaphor.

Two hundred years ago, at the height of European colonial expansion, powerful nations sought to extend their economic domains. During this era explorers entered jungles no European had walked in before. Equally, the tribespeople living in the jungles had never seen white people before. A clash of cultures ensued. The Europeans discovered people they could dominate and resources they could exploit. Some tribes initially welcomed the new arrivals, but as more Europeans followed in the explorers' footsteps, the tribes began to see the incursions as threatening their way of life. Some even saw the newcomers as a source of meat to be thrown into their cooking pots. On both sides threats proliferated, fears grew, and warfare broke out. All this resulted because Europeans crossed the threshold that is the edge of the jungle.

When you cross the threshold of your inner world, something of the same process occurs. You are entering foreign territory—at least, it is foreign to your human you. For others, including incidentally your own spiritual self, it is where they live. It is their home. So you need to be aware that when you cross the inner threshold you are entering others' natural territory. An attitude of respect is always useful in such circumstances. Some of the first wave of colonial explorers certainly maintained an attitude of respect, even humility, when they met native peoples. Unfortunately, this was not shared by the majority of those who followed. As we just noted, fear came to dominate interactions. And mutual destruction followed.

This is a crude representation of what happened when the initial waves of colonial incursions into the territories of native peoples occurred in many places around the world. Of course, the reality was much more complex than this. But it serves as a metaphor to convey something of the situation that applies when you, inhabiting the awareness of your human you, cross the inner threshold and seek to make contact with what inhabits the spiritual realms.

Everyone is initially surprised by what they find. Unless, that is, they have been well instructed by those who in traditional tribal communities are called shamans. Then they have information on what to expect. For everyone else, wherever they travel and whoever they find is a surprise. Surprise naturally leads to fear. Fear is biologically bred into your human you and manifests in the self-preserving behaviours of fight or flight. Socially and psychologically fear manifests as fear of the new, fear of the unknown, fear of the stranger, and so on. Accordingly, that surprise triggers fear is unsurprising. Nor is it surprising that the human imagination, stimulated by that fear, conjures up tales of threatening places, of scary presences, and of evil spirits, all of which further evoke fear in others. This doesn't need to be the response, but too often it is. And those false embroidered tales are passed on from one generation to another. Thus does a taboo come into existence.

So the first emotion you need to overcome when you cross the inner threshold and are confronted by new experiences is the emotion of fear. Fear will transform surprise into panic. And panic will make you turn around and not come back. This is why we have previously emphasised the negative impact of fear and proposed openness as its most useful replacement.

Let's say, then, that you are not troubled by fear, or at least that you are able to set it aside when you encounter something new while meditating. What happens next? Is there really any danger? After all, we just presented a metaphor for incursions into the inner realm in which we mentioned that some living in the jungle felt threatened by the arrival of colonists, while others responded by throwing the Europeans into their cooking pots. Does this happen in the spiritual domains? Are you potentially some spiritual identity's supper? The answer is, no. And yes. We'll explain.

Your spiritual you cannot be eaten by anything on either the physical or spiritual level. Tales to the contrary are entirely imagined. As a spiritual identity you are part of the All that has manifested everything. Eventually, you will merge with that All from which you originally emerged. This will be done willingly and will be hugely satisfying both to you and to the All. Before then you will not be any other identity's supper. However—and yes, we are aware of how many buts and howevers we are offering in this series of answers, entirely because reality is far more complex than human beings normally recognise—there are certain threats to the continued comfort of your human you in excursions into the spiritual domain. An extension of our metaphor will explain how this is so.

When the first explorers entered the world's jungles they exposed themselves to viruses and creatures living in the jungle. Bodies normally develop immunity to viruses common to the environment in which they are raised. But when people enter new physical environments, their bodies may fall ill due to encountering bacteria to which their immune systems have not developed a response. Similarly, insects and parasites like leeches may attach themselves to the explorer's body or lay eggs under their skin. Debilitating physical reactions result. In extreme situations, the body may die. All this is a natural danger when anyone enters a new physical environment. The danger is widely recognised, to the extent that travellers are advised to have inoculations before they visit new countries.

Are these dangers evil? Are bacteria and parasites evil? No. They are just using evolutionarily successful survival strategies. If a leech attaches itself to your skin and sucks your blood, or if a parasite buries eggs in your skin so when its infants hatch they have a source of sustenance, this is not an evil plot hatched against you. It is certainly not happening to punish you. It is just the way nature works. Furthermore, if you are savvy and take precautions, you can avoid the dangers and your body will not be fed on at all.

The same applies when you explore spiritual domains. Non-embodied identities exist that are parasitical in nature. But they do not feed on you at the level of your spiritual you. When you cross the threshold, you may unwittingly attract the attention of a spiritual identity that follows you back when you re-enter your normal state of awareness and attaches itself to you. It doesn't attach itself to your body per se, but to the energetic self associated with your body. It does this to feed, just as a leech attaches itself to your skin to feed. And as is the case with the leech, there is nothing evil or inherently scary about this. Most people are not even aware that the parasitical presence is there, apart perhaps from some tiredness or lethargy, which are usually dismissed as resulting from too much busyness or stress.

The types of energy such identities feed on consists of intense and comparatively crude emotional and sexual energy. Ongoing worry, fear of course, self-pity, and unrelieved sexual desire, are typical types of energy. Naturally, if one doesn't manifest these emotions or energies there is nothing for the parasites to enjoy, so they either leave or are not attracted to you in the first place. This again underlies why we suggest you work on purifying your psychological make-up and transform negative attitudes and emotions into positive traits.

Is there anything to fear when you meditate? No. If when you cross the threshold you possess an open, positive attitude of mind, and have no fear or trepidation, then you are highly unlikely to attract the non-embodied equivalent of a leech. Even if you do, it cannot do serious damage. Where, in extreme cases, jungle viruses can kill your body, non-embodied parasites cannot and do not. Alternatively, discovering that you have such a parasite, and learning how to detach it and send it on its way, may be seen as another skill that it is useful to develop. In the same way that jungle explorers learned how to take care of their body through trial and error, so experience will teach you how to successfully and safely navigate previously unknown spiritual territories.

As regards the question about the existence of demons, they are products of human imagination. There does exist a class of spiritual identities that are mischievous and like to cause a little local mayhem. Mostly, these are deceased, non-embodied human spirits who have not moved on to begin the process of reviewing their just-passed life. Occasionally, they are a non-human identity who is being playful. Any person with mediumistic skills can send them on their way. In fact, just expressing that intent is usually sufficient. They offer no threat.

Those called succubi are exaggerations of the class of parasitical non-embodied identities that feed off repressed sexual energy. It is notable that the term *succubus* originally developed in the Western world among monks who regularly crossed the threshold into the spiritual domain but were also troubled by intense sexual desires. They developed sufficient sensitivity to become aware that identities were feeding on their sexual desires—they were less aware that the guilt they generated regarding their desires was equally attractive to some of those identities. Because of their religious training, they identified the unwanted guests as demons rather than as the psychologically neutral parasites that they actually are.

Lilith is a personification of this religious projection. Throughout history, inner explorers have encountered parasitic identities. Over time, stories of their experiences were combined to form a mythological creature, Lilith. She doesn't exist, of course, being a creation of the human mind. Previously, we observed that each religious and spiritual tradition has created its own cultural stream. Personifications like Lilith are a manifestation of a particular stream. She is a projection of human imagination, the fanciful embroidering of a relationship that has been expanded far beyond its actual circumstance. That a mythological character like Lilith is a human construction is underpinned by the fact that she is female and visits men. She doesn't have a male equivalent who visits women. Why not? Because Lilith represents a cultural stream generated by men. Alert readers will remember our observation that cultural streams function as a conduit between the spiritual and human domains, and so may be used by non-embodied spiritual identities to communicate with embodied human beings. This is also the case with Lilith. We leave those who find this of interest to explore the implications for themselves.

We end by returning to an observation we have already made. After you cross the threshold, it is to your benefit to maintain an open attitude. But there is no benefit in being naive. Feel free to explore, yet remain pragmatic. And know there is nothing to fear.

Question 9

What do I gain from entering the spiritual realm?

That's all very intense. I need to take a step back here, because meditating to find information is one thing, but entering a spiritual realm and encountering identities is something else again—especially when you've compared the spiritual realm to a jungle and said the jungle contains creatures that like to nibble on us. If a spiritual encounter could prove so dangerous, why do it? What do I gain? Why bother?

THE GUIDES RESPOND:

We begin responding to this question by observing that fear is a natural response when faced by new experiences. However, fear also naturally exaggerates dangers, which leads to paralysis. We repeat what we have already stated: there is no danger. What is on offer when you cross the threshold is adventure. As in all adventures, you may fall over and skin your knee, twist an ankle, even break your leg. But the body heals and you carry on. A common saying states, nothing ventured, nothing gained. This is what the situation we are discussing here comes down to. If you allow fear to rule your life choices you will achieve very little in any field of endeavour. Fear is the enemy. Rise above it.

As regards the adventures that become available to you when you cross the threshold and enter what we have likened to the jungle, they are certainly worth commenting on further. As the question points out, obtaining information by learning to listen to subtle streams of thought is a passive activity—passive in the sense that reading a book is passive. Of course, when you listen to subtle streams of thought you need an alert mind and to be engaged and ask questions. However, your awareness remains where it is; it doesn't go wandering.

In contrast, we are now advocating that you actively send your awareness into unknown territories. Compared to listening, this is a much more active approach to gathering information. Yet it also offers experiences that simply cannot be undergone by listening to subtle thoughts. The contrast is similar to the difference between reading a book about a foreign city and travelling to the city and experiencing it for yourself. This is not an entirely accurate comparison, because subtle streams of thought contain experiential riches far deeper than those available when you read a book. So the comparison is crude, but it broadly indicates the difference between the two forms of experience.

What will you encounter when you step over the threshold and enter the non-embodied realm?

First, appreciate that what you encounter depends on you. As a general rule, whoever journeys into the spiritual realm doesn't merely desire to see something new. They are not simply sightseeing. What initiates such a journey is a deep inner call. It is the spiritual self that actually makes the call, although the spiritual self's voice may echo within the essence self, at the emotional or intellectual level, where it is felt as a desire to connect more deeply than is usual for human beings. This echo often gives rise to confusion, and individuals can spend some time coming to terms with the call. Why they answer the call is that embedded in it is a need to know something, feel something, or find something that they passionately consider is important to them. To repeat, the drive behind the call always emanates from the spiritual self. In turn, an individual's spiritual self is drawing their human self's attention to something in their life that is out of sync, or is inharmonious, wrong, needs bolstering, or is simply missing.

We have previously observed that you are only given information about yourself on a need-to-know basis. Only as information becomes significant to you—because you need it to solve a problem, illuminate a difficulty, or require a broader context to understand what is happening—is that information released. It isn't that secrets are arbitrarily withheld, but simply that key information only becomes important to you when you need it to advance. If you received the information too early it would be confusing. Receiving it when you need it ensures it strikes home vividly and tellingly.

The same principle applies to what we are discussing here. Embedded in the call to journey into the spiritual realm is a question, a lack, or a problem to be solved that is germane to your current life situation. So when you respond to the call, gather your inner resources, step over the threshold, and project your awareness into the spiritual domain, you are doing so because you are driven by the need to discover something necessary for your continued growth. It is a next step you feel is urgently required for your evolution as a spiritual being engaged in a series of human incarnations.

One of the most commonly felt reasons for entering the spiritual domain is that explorers wish to encounter the Divine. Whether the Divine is envisaged as a personal being, a particular god-form, a formless field of energy, or a limitless intangible spiritual presence, numerous seekers throughout history have sought a spiritual encounter with what is greater. The motive is usually a passionate desire to transcend the limitations, conflicts and dissatisfactions basic to human existence. In fact, what they are seeking is an encounter with their own spiritual self. As we have already observed, this is the first level of spiritual interaction. And it is a very rich encounter. We'll explain.

Imagine that you had access to an individual who remembers all they went through during hundreds of lifetimes, has collated all their experiences into an archive of knowledge, and has extracted innumerable life lessons from everything they had undergone. Moreover, this individual is not caught up in the hurley burley of daily life but is able to maintain a level of detachment while also being compassionate, understanding and tolerant. Such an individual would certainly be considered wise in human terms. Among the spiritually inclined, such a person is called a guru, an inspired and inspiring teacher.

Now imagine that you can sit at the feet of such a wise one. Moreover, you can close your eyes, quieten your mind, and merge with the deep being of this person, experiencing for yourself everything they have felt and know. The desire to meet and learn from such a wise person motivates people when they go on spiritual quests and pilgrimages, crossing oceans and mountains in the hope that meeting such a person will inspire them in their own journey through life.

You can certainly go on a physical journey to meet such a person. However, what you must know is that a wise person is available to you without physically travelling anywhere. That wise person is your own spiritual self. The inspired and inspiring guru is you. You have lived hundreds of lives. You have gone through multiple experiences. You have a huge stock of life lessons to drawn from. And you don't have to cross oceans or mountains or wait among thousands of other seekers in order to have a personal audience. You are already there. Your spiritual you is already available! All you need do is sit quietly, close your eyes, cross your inner threshold, and encounter your own expansive, transcendent self.

So this is the first level of spiritual identity that is available to you. Given your spiritual self is expansive and accepting and appreciative of what you are doing in this life, and given that human level awareness is so narrow in comparison, when you first encounter your own spiritual self it is a revelatory experience. For many people it feels like an encounter with the Divine. And it is. Because ultimately, to use religious language, you are part of the Divine. All is Divine. To use more neutral language, consciousness is present everywhere and permeates everything and everyone. There is nowhere where consciousness is not. So when you encounter your own consciousness, no matter how revelatory that experience is, it is just your first experience with what exists beyond the human everyday. Much else exists in the spiritual domain, available for you to experience.

Obviously, you are not the only spiritual identity existing in the spiritual domain. Every single human being has their own expansive spiritual self waiting to be contacted, whether by themselves or by others. Similarly, every other living creature around you has a spiritual identity with which it is associated.

Shamans have experienced and teach about the existence of many kinds of spirits that inhibit the middle world, that being the spiritual level directly associated with the physical world. Again, you don't need to travel far to meet these kinds of spirits. The world, the planet Earth, is filled with spirits. Many spirits are associated with physical species, with particular plants and animals. Other spiritual identities are associated with places or natural processes. This is because just as you are a spiritual being who has chosen to enter a human body in order to experience, learn and grow, so other kinds of spiritual beings have chosen to associate themselves with non-human species for exactly the same purpose. If you wish to approach these spirits, you are best doing so in the same way that you would approach a wise guru: with an attitude of humility and a desire to learn. Just like your spiritual self, these spiritual identities have been around a long time and have observed and experienced much. They also know and can do things that are not easily accessed or carried out at the everyday human level. Such interactions can be very valuable for those who wish to understand pets, animals they work with, or creatures that occupy local environments.

The other significant category of spiritual identities are those who are spirit guides. Some people call them angels, although this is an exaggerated term for spiritual identities who are, basically, of the same order of consciousness as you. There are various levels of spirit guides. As we have already explained, some of your guides are members of your close and extended spiritual family. They look out for you when you are embodied, just as you look out for when they are embodied. This is the level of friends and peers. The next level of spirit guides are those who are more experienced, often significantly so. Some among them are approaching the completion of their cycle of incarnation in human form. They function as advisors and teachers. Beyond them are spirit guides who have completed their cycle of incarnation. Each level of spirit guide has access to different forms of knowledge and experience, depending on what they themselves have gone through and learned. Any and all of these are accessible to you, depending on what you ask for and what you need.

Finally, there are many spirits in the spiritual domain that are quite different from those normally associated with earthly activity. You will come to learn of those as and when you wish and need to. There is no point in us saying any more about them for now: they are there for you to discover as you wish. The primary difference between these spiritual identities and your guides is that your guides are invested in your progress, whereas these non-earthly spirits are neutrally engaged. When you come into mutual contact, they are as likely to be curious about you as you are about them.

This is a short answer to your question. We reiterate: the notion that dangers exist in humanity's interactions with spirits is overstated. It is fuelled by fear. There is a chance you may pick up something annoying or do the awareness equivalent of twisting an ankle. Nothing is permanent. It is all part of exploring. And, let's face, just living close to other people in the human domain is no easy ride. Everything you do has its difficulties. And rewards. It's the way life is.

Question 10

Where do extraterrestrials fit in?

You've talked about spirits associated with the Earth and its many species. But what about beings who appear to have arrived here from other planets? I'm talking about extra-terrestrials. Too many people have reported interactions with ETs for them to be ignored. Where do they fit in with us? Are they guides, curious visitors, or do they have their own agenda for being here? Do they ultimately plan to take over?

THE GUIDES RESPOND:

This question contains a number of assumptions. Some are false, while others require adjustment, so we need to present a little contextualising background information before we can answer.

We'll begin by using a model that has been presented elsewhere. Broadly speaking, reality can be said to consist of three basic levels. The first is the electrophysical. This is the physical, bodily level. It includes everything that is apparent to your senses, which you can physically access by touching, seeing, smelling, and so on. The second level is the electromagnetic. Microwaves, x-rays, and the spectrum of light both visible and invisible to human senses exist at the electromagnetic level. The human aura, an aspect of the energetic self, is also electromagnetic. The electromagnetic realm is more rarefied than the electrophysical. More rarefied again is the third, the electrospiritual spectrum. Your spiritual self exists at this level, along with every other spirit.

Within each of the three fundamental levels are further levels. From the human perspective, material forms extend from the everyday to the microscopic to the sub-atomic to the quantum field where matter dissolves. Other forms of matter are much larger than the human, from the planetary, to the galactic, to sheets of billions of galaxies. Some matter takes the form of rocky minerals. Other matter is organic, liquid or gaseous in form. The same variations apply to the electromagnetic spectrum, with frequencies ranging from very large waves to very small waves, and where most frequencies are invisible to other frequencies, so they pass right through each other. The same variation applies to the electrospiritual. Some spiritual identities are huge, others are minute, and identities commonly vibrate on different frequencies, rendering them imperceptible to each other. Human beings function cognitively and perceptually within a very narrow band of what exists physically, electromagnetically and spiritually throughout reality. Much of what is happening occurs outside your powers of perception and understanding. This is one fact you need to consider.

The other fact you need to appreciate is that, from your human perspective, none of the three basic levels exist wholly separate from one another. Every physical entity has an electromagnetic aura as well as a spiritual identity associated with it. While spiritual identities can exist wholly and solely in the spiritual domain, beings living in the physical domain cannot exist without the electromagnetic and the electrospiritual levels. A planet without either would be lifeless.

So from the human perspective it is necessary to appreciate that the three basic levels of reality are intertwined. However, different individuals have varying perceptions and cognition of how this is so. Some perceive other people's auras, and even the auras of trees and mountains. Others can hear those in the spiritual domain, some see them, others can fly out of their body and join them. But even these more perceptually and cognitively able human beings are aware of only a narrow band of the totality of what exists. We repeat, most of exists does so outside the humanly perceptable electrophysical, electromagnetic and electrospiritual bands of reality.

One factor that contributes to this narrowness of human awareness is that what are called extraterrestrial biological beings (EBEs) exist on different frequencies. A way to understand this is to appreciate that fog contains physical molecules just like your body, but they are less dense and are suspended in air. Similarly, many EBEs possess a much more subtle body compared to the human body, consisting of physical molecules that vibrate at a high frequency and possess so little physical density that they are suspended in the electromagnatic. Their bodies may be likened to gas molecules suspended in ultraviolet light. These kinds of EBE bodies don't need to ingest food and drink like the human body requires to continue living, so they don't have respiratory, digestive or excretionary systems. Their body shape is also less defined. Human observers have noted the degree to which some EBEs are able to shapeshift. This is because they project a mental image of themselves to those human beings to whom they chose to appear. The less your awareness is tied to the outright physical, the more your activities are actioned by pure intent, and the less you are tied to a single physical identity.

Throughout the physical universe EBEs exist in a wide range of forms and frequencies, from the incredibly dense, being rock-hard and apparently immobile, to the biological, as on this planet, to what may best be termed ethereal. From the human perspective, being a biological entity involves carbon-based life-forms fuelled by water and light. From our perspective, a biological entity encompasses every type of life-form imaginable, evolved from any and all chemical bases, and living within often inconceivable environments. An example of what we mean exists here on Earth, in the creatures that scientists have discovered living in boiling water heated by undersea volcanic vents. Scientists considered life in such environments impossible—until living creatures were found. The same may be said for life in the universe. It exists in forms and at frequencies within the electrophysical and electromagnetic spectrums that human beings can't currently conceive. Of course, just because they are inconceivable doesn't mean they aren't out there. Or already here.

Are extra-terrestrials a threat to humanity? To respond in the widest sense, every human being living on this planet is an extraterrestrial, because all originate from the spiritual domain. You, and every other human being, migrated to this planet in order to inhabit human bodies. The same applies to all the other varieties of spirits who have migrated here to associate with non-human biological species. Just because human spiritual identities have been inhabiting this planet for a very long time doesn't make you any less of an extraterrestrial.

As regards the biggest threat to the planet, it doesn't come from invading ETs but from humanity. Over-population, factory farming and fishing, pollution of the land, air and sea, predatory commerce, devastation of habitats, extermination of species, war-mongering, the threat of devastation via nuclear technology ... human beings pose the biggest threat to themselves and to the planet. If ETs did invade and take over, they could hardly do a worse job of caring for the planet and all those living on it! We are joking, of course. We don't foresee ETs actually invading and taking over. This is merely another fear human beings project onto reality.

What we have tried to indicate in our answer is that reality is much more complex, and the presence of identities on, in and around this planet is much more nuanced, than current human assumptions take into account. As to what will happen in the future, what interactions will develop between these many kinds of electrophysical, electromagnetic and electrospiritual identities, and how the very real threats to the planet's current status will be resolved ... only time will tell.

How can I contact people in the spiritual realm?

Earlier you outlined how we can use meditation to obtain information from the spiritual realm. How do I use meditation to initiate contact with identities existing in the spiritual realm? Can I even initiate contact, or is it more that I need to open myself up and wait for the identities to contact me? Are there rules of engagement? What's the go with direct contact?

THE GUIDES RESPOND:

This is an interesting question all round. It's interesting to you because you wish to learn about the possibility of having experiences beyond what are normal in human life. And it is interesting to us because we are also always seeking to extend our experience and knowledge. Without new contacts, without new experiences, knowledge doesn't expand and growth doesn't take place.

On these grounds it might be thought that no one would seek to avoid new contacts. Yet this isn't the case. While making new contacts was essential to you during your early years, because it helped you learn skills, such as how to talk and how to behave in conformity with your community's norms, by the time people become adult they have set situations they prefer to spend time in and established ways of interacting with others. In general, after human beings reach adulthood they become quite conservative in who they seek out for personal contact. So being open and inviting unknown identities into your awareness is a significant step. No one does it lightly. There has to be a deeply felt need that drives you to move out of your established patterns of behaviour, out of your comfort zone, to seek contact with what can quite accurately be termed the unknown.

To be motivated to initiate contact with any spiritual identity you require a need of some kind. Often it is a question you want answered. Or it may also be an experience you want to have—such as the desire to interact with the Divine, on which we commented previously. It could be said that you seek contact because there is something in it for you, something sufficiently important that you are encouraged to break through the psychological factors that hold you back from initiating contact with the unknown.

An unsolved question or need commonly provides the impetus to seek contact. It is a set pattern that everyone who wishes to contact those existing beyond the physical shares this motivation. However, what happens next, how actual contact occurs, has no set pattern. One reason is because different people have different levels of prior experience. For some contact is established quickly and easily. Others who have little prior experience (we're referring to past life experience) will have to work hard to develop their communication skills— because establishing a line of communication between yourself and non-embodied spiritual identities is a skill that must be learned. Everyone also has their own innate propensities, which take the form of preferences and previously developed abilities. So communication will always occur in a way that fits with what you already know, what you can already do, and what you feel comfortable engaging with.

For example, in times long ago, when human beings lived off the land by harvesting plants, fishing and hunting, they were highly attuned to the natural world. People were also brought up to believe that everything in the world, animate and inanimate, was filled with spirits. Accordingly, when communications with spiritual identities occurred, the spirits were thought of as taking the form of nature spirits and animals which possessed powers beyond the human, from whom human beings could learn. This is the basis of shamanic interactions with those in the spiritual realm. In more recent times religions have taught people to conceive of spirits as angels, deceased saints, and human-like gods. In order to open up a channel of communication with spiritual identities you need to have a clear idea of what the spiritual is to you. After all, if you doubt the existence of spirits, or what is more common, if you doubt that you have the ability or the right to converse with spiritual identities, that doubt is a barrier which will stop you from achieving communication.

So to initiate contact you require, first, a question or need, and second, a context for thinking about the spiritual realm. We suggest that a metaphor for the spiritual realm appropriate for the modern age is that of vast, open interstellar space. Interstellar space is mostly empty, with stars, solar systems and galaxies a long way off. Similarly when, during meditation, you first cross the threshold and look out, the inner realm appears black, vast and empty. Extending the metaphor, many television shows have been produced according to the premise that interstellar space contains non-human species, technologies and civilisations, each of whom follow their inclinations and strive to achieve their own goals. We offer the idea that spiritual space echoes interstellar space precisely because it is similarly filled with non-human identities who are focused on living their own experiences, who have their own modes for interacting, who set their own goals, and who follow their own inclinations. The comparison could even be extended to include the notion that just as the starship Enterprise is an interstellar explorer, boldly going where no other human beings have gone before, so you are potentially a spiritual explorer, going where you have not been before—at least, not in this life.

The final point we would make in relation to this metaphor is that the interstellar explorer doesn't pre-judge what is found, and certainly doesn't try to fit non-human beings into a religious schemata, adjudging this being an angel, that a demon, that a god. Rather, interstellar explorers adopt more of an anthropological approach, being curious regarding what non-human beings are and how they live. In just the same way, you are best advised to be open-minded in your spiritual explorations and not squeeze what you encounter into pre-formed schemata. You should certainly not jump to judgemental conclusions.

So then, with your personal question or need identified, and given you now have a contextualising metaphor to hold in mind that encourages you to sustain an open attitude towards the spiritual realm, we return to the question: how do you actually make contact? For the reasons we have already outlined, we repeat there is no set way that contact with spiritual identities is made. However, we can offer some examples.

In the case of our scribe working on these pages, contact was initiated via writing. To contextualise this, an extensive history exists of people using automatic writing to communicate with spiritual identities. This is done by the individual projecting a question, clearing his or her mind to establish a quiet, meditative state, and waiting for an answer to enter the subconscious part of the mind, which in turn stimulates the motor system, whereon the response is automatically written. Other people use Tarot cards or cards marked according to some other occult system as a way to communicate with spiritual identities. Throughout history, tea leaves, sticks, dice and all kinds of objects have also been used. In each case, the individual has to establish a quiet meditative inner state so the spiritual identity's subtle communication may be heard. In each case, intent initiates contact.

Our scribe's process is a variation on these practices. At first, as he edited a colleague's written channelled communications, he intended to make contact by deliberately opening himself up to guidance from those who had initiated his colleague's writing. Gradually, as responses to his questions about editing came to him via dreams and subtle impressions while working, he became convinced that spiritual identities were available for personal contact. After almost four years of this process, he had opened his mind sufficiently, and sufficiently tuned in to the requisite energy level, that a subtle stream of thought became apparent to him. Thus contact was established. Contact continues, as the existence of this text affirms.

Other people use prayer to open themselves up and tune into contact. Still others use chanting, drumming or dancing. Some ingest psychedelics. Others use trance, lucid dreaming, out-of-body travelling, or develop their extra-sensory perceptions. Common to every one of these practices is that practitioners learn to enter a quiet, meditative inner state. So it can be said that meditation underpins all communication practices, even those that are outwardly noisy and full of physical movement.

Accordingly, with regard to the question of how meditation may be used to make contact with spiritual identities, the answer is that you must find a practice that suits you and your sensibility. Whatever practice you are drawn towards, it will appeal because it fits with skills you have previously developed and because it suits your social conditioning, psychological temperament and life situation. So feel free to look around. But don't over-think your choice. Select a practice not by thinking about it but in silence. Then you will feel the subtle—or perhaps it won't be subtle at all—push towards the practice that is most appropriate for you.

Throughout everything you do, your inner attitude is crucial. You need to be wary of the tricks of your gloopy self. In spiritual teachings practitioners are warned against allowing their ego into what they do, to be wary of powerful traits such as vanity, arrogance or lust for power. We prefer the more general term of gloopy self to that of ego, because in fact all kinds of psychological traits come into play in spiritual endeavours, just as they do in everyday life.

One reason is that when you draw on an ability you developed in previous lives, it is highly likely that negative and self-limiting traits are also associated with that ability, due to their being generated at the same time as the ability and so become embedded in it. Consequently, they will seep into whatever activity you are using the ability for in this life. This often occurs without your being aware of it. So we advise you to keep watch on your inner state.

In particular, be aware of agitation, of lines of thinking and feeling that depart from a quiet inner state. Don't ignore or suppress them, because that would merely allow them to run rampant at a sub-conscious level. Rather, give them attention. Detach from them, observe where they go inside you, what they ignite, and what behaviours they trigger. You will learn much about yourself if you are able to follow linked agitated emotions and thoughts. Especially be wary of feelings and thoughts that rise either during or after your spiritual journeying. They will taint your attitude when you make contact with spiritual identities. An agitated state will likely cause them to withdraw until you have inwardly sorted yourself out.

The question was asked if you should initiate contact, or if you should instead create an open inner state, then wait for spiritual identities to contact you. The fact is either can and does work. If you have a question, do what you can to find the answer. Initiate what contacts you need, with both human beings and spiritual identities. Make the most of whatever opportunity is available to you. On the other hand, sometimes spiritual identities initiate contact without you feeling you asked for it. This may be because your life plan includes such contact, which means you agreed to it between lives. As a result, your spiritual you planned the contact, and the situation is just that you at your human level aren't aware of the plan. Additionally, sometimes soul friends initiate contact to help you in trying times or when you are struggling to make a crucial decision. Such contacts also occur with the agreement of your spiritual you, because those making contact are your friends, and friends help each other out when one is in a bind. So even contacts that seem not to be initiated by you almost always involve your agreement at a spiritual and pre-life level.

Finally, the question was asked if rules of engagement apply to interactions with spiritual identities. Yes, absolutely. Being humble and grateful, and not falling into the trap of assuming you know more than you do, is always helpful. So is being curious and questioning what is happening. We don't mean being sceptical, although a pinch of scepticism is useful. What we mean by suggesting you keep questioning is to think about whatever you find from a variety of perspectives. Don't take anything at face value. Try to understand how a single event, perception or piece of knowledge fits into a wider context. Keep trying to fill in the gaps in your understanding. Shine a light into what you haven't perceived, and never settle for easy explanations. Subtle experiences are always complex from a human perspective. So constantly push and probe. And maintain awareness of your inner changing states, sustaining a self-critical attitude.

These aren't rules in the human sense of rules you must conform to or else you'll be punished. These are rules in a much more open sense, that you need to learn to work with to maximise your opportunities. At times you'll certainly make mistakes and screw up opportunities. But that happens during any learning process.

The difference between making mistakes in the human world and making mistakes at the spiritual level is that the human world can be brutal on those who make mistakes, but those in the spiritual realm will never punish you for your errors. What happens instead is that the mistake goes into the box with everything else you learn through life, good and not so good. Learning contact by contact, experience by experience, you'll consolidate your knowledge, grow more capable, and become ever more able to handle whatever comes your way.

Question 12

Are chakras more like telephone lines or doorways?

What about chakras? Does purifying and strengthening them help us communicate with spiritual identities? Are chakras like telephone lines that connect us so we can speak to spiritual identities? Or are they more like doorways that open up directly into the spiritual realm?

THE GUIDES RESPOND:

Before answering these questions about chakras, we need to clarify the context. As a human being you have an energetic self, which includes your aura and other electromagnetic aspects of your being. When you were in the womb the aura provided a template that generated your body shape at a cellular level. Now, as a mature human being, the aura facilitates communication between those in the spiritual realm and you living in the human realm. The chakras are another part of the interconnective electromagnetic complex that contributes to your energetic self.

Simply, chakras are energy centres, energy fulcrums if you like. They exist on the electromagnetic level but are also associated with specific areas of the body. Historically, differing systems for describing the charkras have developed in different cultures. The Chinese refer to five chakras, the Indians to seven and the Jewish Kabbalah to twelve, although in the last case this is also a metaphysical system, designed to relate the micro human to the macro cosmic. Here we will adhere to the Indian descriptive system of seven chakras. We do so not because it is more truthful, but simply on pragmatic grounds, because it is the most widely known chakra system in today's English-speaking world.

Different traditions emphasise different chakras. For those practising martial arts, the chakra situated just below the belly button is key. Among those who practise Tantra and Taoist sex magic, the sex centre chakra is a focus. For those dedicated to prayer, the heart chakra is central. For meditators, the solar plexus, heart or forehead chakras are the focus, depending on what their practice involves.

There is no hierarchy among practices. One practice is not better than another. Any can be practised, and is practised, by those who are more experienced and able, having lived more lives and having spent more time developing their skills. Similarly, no chakra is more significant or more important than any other. Each has its functions, and each will be cultivated by you during your full incarnation cycle.

The question has been asked, do you need to cultivate your chakras in order to contact those in the spiritual domain? Yes, chakra cultivation is required. But perhaps not in the way you expect. It is useful to look at your existence from an energetic perspective. We previously discussed EBEs and observed that they exist in a range of frequencies, from the very dense to the ethereal. This range also applies to human awareness.

Most people's awareness is focused on their immediate physical reality. That is what they pay most attention to—which is entirely appropriate, because that is what you incarnate to do. But people engage with the physical in different ways. Some live a violent life, applying physical dominance over others, while others dedicate themselves to nurturing other people. It can readily be deduced that this range of behaviours gives rise to different qualities of awareness. Those who are violently domineering possess a denser, more opaque awareness, while those who nurture others possess a comparatively more translucent awareness. The first is like a blunt hammer while the second is more like a cheesecloth, allowing interactions to flow back and forth. However, the comparison isn't quite this straightforward, because among those who prefer to use blunt force, some are more subtle in how they apply it. Possessing insight into human psychology, they cunningly use persuasive tactics that get around their victim's defensive mechanisms. They also employ other people to do their dirty work. Among those who nurture others, some conceive of nurture in rigid terms, putting those in their charge into an inflexible hierarchical framework. Other nurturers are much more fluid and responsive to individual needs and situations. So among nurturers, as among the violently domineering, there is a wide range of quality of engagement, from more rigid to more responsive, and a corresponding range of individual awareness, from heavier to lighter, and from being fixed to being supple.

But this still isn't all. Further complicating this picture is that what may be termed dark storms pass through each individual human awareness from time to time. It happens that occasionally, pressured by people and events in the local environment, an individual reacts via their gloopy self and becomes negatively immersed in whatever is happening to them and around them. As a result, that individual's awareness becomes denser than is usual for a shorter or longer period. The opposite also occurs. A human being's awareness is quite capable of becoming lighter and more sensitive than is normal for it, also for shorter or longer periods. As would be expected, less dense states of awareness involve greater sensitivity, which in turn facilitates contact with those in the subtle spiritual realm.

Chakras certainly play a role in your achieving more sensitive states of awareness. Therein lies their significance. However, in order to appreciate their role, we need to fill out the picture of your energetic self a little more. Like your biological self—our term for your body complex—your energetic self possesses a range of interconnected systems, each with its own sets of functions. Physically, your body's nervous system has an endocrine network, which regulates organs, while your brain is a complex networked system that processes sense perceptions using its limbic system and cognitive capacities. If either are impaired, for example through physical trauma or starvation, a knock-on effect occurs, functions and capacities are impacted, and the biological self's overall functioning falls below what is normal. The same applies to your energetic self. Being a complex of interconnected energy centres, when one centre is not functioning normally it impacts on other centres. Two factors in particular affect chakra functioning.

The first is that human existence is so full of conflict, and so often requires self-defensive manoeuvring, hardly anyone's energetic network functions to its optimal capacity. In previous centuries, when mystics withdrew from everyday life and lived in a monastery, ashram or zendo, and when, in even earlier times, mystics withdrew to live in the wilderness, personal conflict was minimised and consequently it was easier to live an energetically balanced lifestyle. The modern lifestyle is not only not conducive to energetic balance, its pressures actively promote imbalance. How does one develop balance? There are two approaches: from the outside and from the inside.

Rebalancing from the outside most commonly occurs when an individual visits a healer who is capable of retuning the chakras. To offer one example, as a result of negative emotions an individual feels in response to events in the outside world, the chakra in the solar plexus can become depressed. By applying energy in a spiral motion the chakra can be retuned and brought back up to a level of normal functioning. At times, those in spirit may also perform this healing function, retuning depressed chakras to help those in their charge rebalance.

These external applications of chakra retuning are useful immediate fixes. However, in the long-term it is better for each individual to learn to readjust their chakras themselves, from the inside. Meditation offers a useful method for doing so, simply by inviting in reviving energy that you direct towards a particular chakra. Sometimes the energy comes from the individual's spiritual self, and sometimes from a non-embodied guide who is aiding progress. It doesn't matter what the source is, just that the chakra is re-energised. Of course, it would be best if the chakra wasn't depleted in the first place. What depletes it is engaging with the mechanisations of the gloopy self. Working against your own negative and self-limiting attitudes and behaviours will help keep your chakras in robust health, reducing your need for remedial attention in the first place.

The second principal factor that impacts on the functioning of chakras is personal fixation. As we mentioned earlier, different traditions tend to focus on specific chakras. Martial arts focus on the belly button chakra, religious worship focuses on the heart chakra, and some forms of meditation on the forehead chakra, otherwise known as the third eye, and so on. What happens is that people practising a particular tradition dedicate themselves to that chakra. As they practice they receive feedback from their efforts in the form of heightened states. As a consequence, and whether they are conscious of it or not, their attention becomes fixated on a particular chakra. This is understandable, because they are getting what they experience as serious spiritual action, so it is natural that they continue to focus their efforts on the chakra where that action is happening. The upshot is that they end up in an unbalanced energetic state, with one chakra functioning intensely and at a very high level and the others largely being ignored.

How is remedial rebalancing applied in such a situation? Sometimes individuals are prompted to change their focus. For example, it is common for people who initially grounded their spiritual practices in prayer to later adopt meditation. They shift their focus from the heart chakra to the forehead chakra. But what is more usually the case is that individuals get fixated on a single form of practice for a lifetime. They generate balance by pursuing different practices in subsequent lives, in each of which they focus on a single chakra. In this way they progressively open up and optimise the functioning of all the chakras.

We reiterate, opening the chakras facilitates contact with the spiritual realm. That is the purpose of doing so. In effect, as you learn to connect your awareness with your aura and the network of energy centres that collectively constitute your energetic self, you raise your awareness into a more sensitive state and so become more capable of receiving subtle communications. Nobody achieves a highly sensitive state in fifty lifetimes, let alone in one. So this is one of the tasks you engage in from life to life.

To return to the metaphor we offered earlier, the progress you make can be likened to entering the jungle. In one life you focus on one chakra, let's say situated just below the belly button. The first time you do so, very likely through martial activity or in competitive physical sports, you develop it a little. In other words, you progress a little way into the jungle, opening up a short track. In a subsequent life—it may not be the very next one—you repeat the focus and develop your chakra's potential a little more. This extends your track into the jungle a little further. Life by life, you advance the gains made during previous lives, become more proficient in using that chakra. As a consequence, you forge a track that is progressively wider and travels deeper into the jungle. Then in a subsequent life you use a different practice, let's say prayer, to develop the heart chakra. Again, incrementally, through repeated effort, you forge a new track into the jungle. With each life, as the tracks you create become wider and deeper, you find it progressively easier to enter the jungle. Your previous efforts result in a growing ease of entry. Of course, what you are doing is creating energetic pathways your awareness may use to explore the spiritual realm and contact those dwelling there.

As you approach the end of your incarnational cycle, you will have forged a number of energetic paths into the spiritual domain, along which you can easily travel. Some of your preferred paths will correspond to preferred chakras. This is because while all your energy centres will be developed, personal predilections lead people to prefer one or two over the others. Additionally, the development of individual skills results in people forging different paths. Two examples are an energetic path used to contact deceased people, such as mediums foster, and a verbal communicative channel that channellers establish. Because choice always applies, individuals focus on what most appeals to them. The result is that many different pathways have been opened up between the human world and the spiritual domain.

Does purifying and developing the chakras help you contact spiritual identities? Yes, absolutely. Purification involves working to minimise and eventually eliminate the negativity and self-limiting behaviours enacted by your gloopy self. While developing the chakras is a multi-life task, you have to start somewhere, some time. Everything you do by way of spiritual practice adds to their development. Together, purification and development lead to the incremental fine-tuning of the energy network that comprises your energetic self, a fine-tuning you carry with you from life to life.

Are chakras more like telephone lines or doorways? As you would likely expect, the answer is they function as both. Your energetic self is capable of acting in both ways, and does. You receive spiritual communications via dreams and in the form of fleeting impressions that contain information and inspirational content. At such times, your energetic network acts as a kind of telegraphic transmitter, receiving subtle communications and passing them on to your awareness. In other situations, when your awareness extends out from your body, say via your forehead chakra, that chakra functions as a doorway, opening up non-physical vistas for exploration.

We conclude by making the case that there is no need to become fixated on your chakras. Especially, don't beat yourself up by feeling that you aren't doing enough to purify and develop them. As will be clear from what we have said in these pages, being human is complex, there is a vast amount to deal with, and even the most developed and focused people living in the most conducive situations rarely complete everything they planned for a lifetime. In addition, different lives have different purposes. Chakra development isn't pursued in each and every life. When it is time to focus on a chakra, that requirement will become apparent to you.

In the meantime, and without you being aware of it, many of your actions are indeed contributing to your chakra purification and growth. This is because you already possess an energetic self and an energetic network, and anything you do, whatever choice you make, whichever negative situations you don't engage with, and whichever self-limiting opportunities you rise above, it all resonates within you energetically. As a result of your efforts to become a better, stronger, more complete human being, you are also raising your overall energetic vibration and refining your awareness. So whether you can feel it or not, you *are* working on your chakras. It is an unavoidable consequence of human existence.

Our final observation is that while you are refining your awareness life by life, making it ever more capable of receiving subtle communications, meditation enables you to raise your energetic level higher than is normal. Even though this higher level is only temporary, meditation helps you raise the energy level of your awareness so it may become more sensitive. As a result, you become increasingly able to perceive what, in your ordinary everyday state of awareness, you do not.

Question 13

Do I need to ask
for protection?

Previously you said that when we explore the spiritual domain we run the risk of attracting parasites that feed on our energy. You also said we shouldn't be naive. This implies that when I meditate I should be realistic and protect myself energetically. Is this so? If it is, what works? Should I ask others to protect me? Or can I protect myself?

THE GUIDES RESPOND:

As in all situations where problems arise and defensive action is required, there is no one-size-fits-all answer to your question. Different situations, and particularly different personalities, require different solutions. So we can immediately answer, yes, energetic protection is appropriate. Just as you use sunblock when going out so as not to burn your skin, so you are advised to ensure that when you finish meditating nothing extraneous is clinging to you. Using protection is merely common sense. What is not so apparent is what is best for you in a particular situation.

As a general exercise, it is useful to do what many meditators are taught, which is to imagine an envelope of pure light surrounding you, then envisage it as providing a protective layer, a kind of spiritual prophylactic. Another common practice is to direct a plea towards your spiritual friends and guides to protect you during meditation. Each of these practices is to be encouraged, as they are certainly effective in many, even most, situations. So by all means do one or both before or after your meditation sessions.

However, there is more to parasites than we have discussed so far. In particular, the use of creative visualisation in your spiritual practices, such as imagining your body being enveloped by protective light, requires further explanation. We'll begin with this topic.

In times past the spiritual realm was conceived of as imaginal, a word derived from *image*. Images have long been associated with visions perceived by mystics in what, as a consequence, were termed visionary states. We prefer to say that when people cross the threshold to explore the spiritual realm, they are entering a visionary realm that is imaginal in nature. The imaginal is a complex concept. As we keep repeating, perhaps annoyingly so, what you are going through as a spiritual identity, occupying a human body and coping with human cultures while simultaneously trying to understand what is occurring to you spiritually, involves an extremely complex psychospiritual situation. We introduce the term *imaginal* here in an attempt to illuminate how you connect with spiritual reality.

The imaginal isn't limited to visions. It includes deep feelings, fleeting impressions, and illuminating intuitions, none of which are necessarily visual in nature—although they could be—and which come from you don't know where to provide revealing nuances and perspectives of which you were previously unaware.

It is the case that many people consider such perceptions to be imagined rather than imaginal. They view the imaginal as entirely conjured up in the mind of the experiencer. For those who are sceptical of imaginal communications—which includes many who have actually experienced them—they are so subtle and so fleeting, and speak in such a quiet voice (we mean this metaphorically, of course), that they are easily discarded, often without the individual thinking twice about what has occurred. This is a completely understandable response among those who have never delved into the imaginal realm of experience, or who have been startled by an unsought imaginal experience and were too confused about what was happening, too doubtful of its source, or too fearful of its consequence, to give it serious consideration. As we said earlier, in general people need a reason to engage with subtle impressions. Furthermore, training is required not just to become sensitised to their occurrence, but to process what they mean. Mistakes in interpretation are frequent. Imagination does play a significant part in misinterpretation. So the difference between the imaginal and the imagined needs to be made clear.

Human imagination has two key applications. First there are those who imagine things that aren't there, such as plots by others to attack them in some way. These people are called paranoid. Their imagination is fuelled by fear, which leads them to interpret otherwise innocent actions as being dangerous to them. This is one example of how imagination fuelled by something else—in this case fear—takes over a person's psyche and conjures a view of reality that is not actually the case.

But human beings also use their imagination creatively, envisaging possibilities that they then bring into existence. Engineers imagine a bridge, an architect imagines a building. They then carry out the tasks needed to build what they have imagined and make it an existing object. Where the paranoid imagination conjures up a world that doesn't exist, except within their mind, the creative imagination drives human progress. These are the two principle ways imagination is used by human beings. But there is a third application.

A widely shared maxim states that you aren't paranoid if they really are out to get you. This is true. But let's dig into that saying a little further. If others are indeed out to get you, then that is because you engaged in a chain of actions and reactions that has resulted in them wanting to do so. Whether you merely responded to what was already occurring, or whether you initiated what subsequently became a chain of events, you made the choice to engage. Others noticed your engagement and responded by coming to get you, whether that be legally, economically, politically or personally. On both sides of the pursuit—you as pursued, them as pursuers—engagement has occurred. How did you engage? By using your creative imagination.

Let's imagine a scenario in which you see things happening you don't like, perhaps by offending your moral sensibility, and you envision an alternative way life could be. As a result, you engage with what you don't like, your purpose being to interrupt what is occurring. In effect, you wish to change the course of future events so you take action to make this happen. This is creative engagement. Your pursuers in turn respond to whatever you do by using their creative imagination to envision that life would be better if they sustained their current course of action. Accordingly, they push back.

The process of creatively imagining how things could be, then engaging to make that imagined possibility real, is fundamental to human existence. It is responsible for the tremendous advances that have been made in recent centuries, socially, technologically, ethically, educationally, medically. It is also responsible for the huge messes humanity makes when the creative imagination is used to exploit and oppress. People see even the most straightforward of situations in very different ways because they possess diverse assumptions, desires and expectations. Competing visions commonly give rise to disagreements, clashes, and fights. In all cases, people's differently aligned creative imaginations are responsible. With this understanding of how creative imagination functions in life, we'll now consider how the use of creative imagination applies to imaginal experiences.

When you imagine an envelope of protective light surrounding you—the colours of either white or gold are suggested—you are using your creative imagination. That is, the envelope of light isn't actually there. Instead, you are envisioning it being there, just like an engineer looks at a gorge and envisions a bridge crossing it. The engineer then uses practical processes to bring the bridge into existence, in ways that are clear and widely appreciated. In contrast, the imaginal process by which envisioned white light comes to actually surround a meditating individual does not involve anything physical, and is neither clearly nor widely appreciated. This is the way with the spiritual layers of reality. They involve real outcomes, but they are subtle, non-physical outcomes, and so difficult to comprehend.

What happens is that by directing your attention towards the spiritual domain and envisioning an envelope of light, you are extending an invitation. Your invitation leads to a response. Often it is your spiritual self that responds, by creating an energetic envelope around you. More precisely, it adds an energetic quality to the envelope that already surrounds you, because your aura envelopes your body from before its birth to after its death. In this case, it may be said you are energising your aura yourself. Occasionally, your invitation results in a separate spiritual identity adding protective energy to your aura. This is usually a mentor or friend coming to your aid. Very occasionally, someone outside your familial and peer circles will help you, for reasons you will likely not know until after your incarnation is complete.

This, then, is how your awareness uses creative imagination to generate imaginal effects. You creatively visualise a state of reality, open yourself up to a subtle result, and that result indeed comes to be. However, imaginal impressions are so ephemeral in comparison to physical reality that they are often felt to hover on a borderline between what is real and what is merely imagined, between what is actually present and what is not. This is the tricky aspect of imaginal perceptions, an aspect spiritual explorers usually take some time to comprehend.

When spiritual explorers first start receiving impressions from the spiritual domain those impressions are elusive. Seekers aren't certain they have actually perceived anything at all. The situation is analogous to perceiving gossamer, which are very fine webs spun by small spiders. Gossamer webs are so fine and delicate you often can't see them. It is only when dew has settled on them, and sunlight catches the droplets, that you realise a web actually hangs before you. It takes looking from a certain perspective, with the right illumination, to realise a web is present. Otherwise you could walk through the web, think you feel something brush your arm, look down, see nothing, and shrug off the impression as merely being your imagination at play.

The same applies to imaginal impressions. You need to see them from a certain angle, in a particular light, to perceive them at all. Otherwise you'll likely shrug them off as being your imagination at play. Imaginal impressions have a visionary, dreamlike quality. Sometimes they strike you powerfully. More usually they are tantalising whispers that you have to concentrate on to hear. Given the lack of physical confirmation, it is easy to rationalise them away as imagined. In fact, you need to switch off your imagination to perceive the imaginal. You do this by stilling your mind and opening up your awareness. Then what are initially felt to be quiet, distant impressions come closer, and the subtle and ephemeral starts being perceived.

In energetic terms, what you are doing is lifting your awareness to a more refined level, until you resonate at the same energetic level as the imaginal. It is when you are on the same wavelength that the imaginal becomes apparent. All this takes practice. Through repeated effort you become more proficient at switching your awareness to the required energetic level, and as a result ephemeral imaginal impressions become increasingly accessible and real to you.

At this stage, however, another difficulty presents itself. This is that imagination can embroider what is perceived. This is common within religions, when some important individual has put a particular interpretation on an imaginal event. Usually a sound intent lies behind the interpretation, such as when a mystic visionary attempts to explain an ephemeral experience using a metaphor drawn from everyday life. Others then misinterpret the explanation, most often by adopting the metaphor as a literal truth. Occasionally, people are mischievous and invent fantastical explanations.

In your own exploring, be careful how you explain what you perceive, not just to others but to yourself. As we have previously warned, easy explanations, made using what you already know, are not necessarily correct explanations. Reality is more diverse, contains a wider variety of processes, and is often far stranger, than anything you can know. Ultimately, the imaginal is far beyond what you could ever imagine. So be careful about projecting what you know onto what you do not. The explanations we are offering here, and in our other books and channelled information, are attempts to give you a fresh context for appreciating what is mysterious and arcane.

As for there being more to parasites than we have so far discussed, much learning awaits you as you repeatedly enter the spiritual domain. There will be surprises. There will be times when you don't believe what you have encountered. And there will be occasions when you ask yourself, "What the (bleep) was that!"

This is entirely natural. It is also what makes exploration so fascinating. If we already knew everything, how insipid life would be. Parasites are of this same order of surprises. They are not simply bugs, like leeches, to be shrugged off. They have their own intelligence and perceptions. They have been many places. Because they exist spiritually, yet interact with the physical energetically—as you do, but in a different way—they have their own view of reality. Furthermore, you can talk to them and ask them all about it. So when you discover an energetic parasite has attached itself to you, while the temptation is to remove it as soon as possible, entering first into communication might be informative for you.

The last comment we will make regarding parasites is that the experience of removing one is an important learning experience. You'll need to draw on resources you perhaps didn't realise you had. It is, as is said, more grist to the mill as you work to grow.

Question 14

What about cling-ons, pick-ups, and negative energy?

I'm not letting you get away with that bland explanation. I've felt an entity hanging around me, influencing me. How can another powerful mindset have that much impact, transforming someone from rational to irrational? Invasive entities have driven people to crime or even mad. It's scary. How can this be allowed? Can these entities even derail our life plan? I want you to explain what's going on. How about starting by defining the nature of entities, cling-ons and pick-ups, and how negative energy contributes to the whole horrible mess?

THE GUIDES RESPOND:

When you discover that an identity is feeding off you energetically, it may be disconcerting, even scary. We acknowledge this. It is similar to being told by a doctor that you have a disease that will take some time to treat, and that you are going to be uncomfortable at times during the treatment cycle.

Different people respond to such news in different ways, depending on their personality. Some get depressed, others become angry, resign themselves to what is happening, or feel resentment that they are being hard done by. Anger can be a powerful motivating force, because it fuels the desire to overcome the situation that has arisen. The need, however, is not to become lost in the anger to the extent that you are paralysed by it, but to channel the anger and use its energy to change your circumstances.

You are right to introduce the concept of negative energy to a consideration of this type of occurrence. Controlling negative energy is crucial to making progress in any life situation. What leads to negative energy becoming a problem in your life is when it is used to fuel the creative imagination. Then, psychologically speaking, all hell can break loose. Perhaps this sounds as scary as an identity being attached to you and siphoning off energy? It should do, because it is often what creates the situation in which a parasitical identity finds you in the first place. This is another situation that varies according to situation and personality.

Everyone creates the major circumstances of their life. Love, work and your preferred forms of play are key aspects of your life plan. You select specific life conditions, including parents, social conditions, country, language, and cultural norms, and you establish major signposts that will occur in your life along the way, You also choose the key people you will interact with. This all happens before you are born. So the major aspects of your current life have been created by you. This ability to create continues into your life. You can make new choices that cause you to depart from what you decided you would do this time round. You can change your plan.

Changes are possible because psychologically you have a great deal of power. You may think that it is your spiritual you that decides, in the midst of a life, that you want to do something else, or go off with someone else, and so not follow the plan you decided on prior to being born. Sometimes this is so. But usually other factors are influential. In particular, your current psychological make-up can be a crucial factor in initiating any diversion you make during the course of your life.

Let's be clear, we certainly don't condemn anyone who diverges from their life plan. Everything you do provides experience, and entering a body and living a life is all about acquiring experience to grow. So there is nothing wrong with diverging from your life plan. Diversions may last weeks, months, or years before individuals have their fill and return to pursing their life plan. Or an entire life plan may be jettisoned. None of this is a mistake. People learn from all experiences. So whatever is taken up or avoided is just more grist to the mill.

There are many reasons why people take diversions from their life plan. They may get diverted by a situation that looks intriguing. Love and sex certainly divert people. So does fear, which stops people following through on what was planned. Occasionally life circumstances prevent individuals from enacting significant aspects of their life plan, such as when a key participant accidentally dies, making it impossible for long-planned activities to take place. This happens. In each case nothing is lost, because new factors come into play from which you can equally learn. Among these diverting factors one in particular is relevant to this topic, that being negative energy.

Each person generates negative energy. The basis of all negative energy is fear, but over time secondary emotions become overlaid on top of the fear, hiding it. We have discussed this in the *Channelled Spirituality* series, so won't spend time on it now. The point is that negative emotions, such as greed, resentment and anger, are by far the greatest source of negative energy for human beings.

Negative emotions arise out of your reactions to life circumstances, and especially your reactions to what other people do to you. If people allow particular incidents or people to dominate their outlook, they end up carrying that emotional reaction long-term, even through the rest of their lives. These negative emotions—other examples are resentment, self-pity, jealousy, vanity—can so dominate an indiviual's psychological make-up that they taint everything they feel. It is like an emotional headset that covers their eyes, ears and mouth and so colours everything they see, hear and say. When a negative emotion is felt intensely for an extended period of time, or when a single traumatic incident drives deep into an individual's psyche, that negative emotion is then transformed into negative energy. How this happens is straightforward.

Everyone has an energetic self, part of which is an electromagnetic envelope of energy that extends around their body. Your energetic self's overall vibration is a reflection of what you are inside yourself. The emotions you commonly emanate, the desires that fuel you, the thoughts you consistently involve yourself with, are reflected in your energetic self. This means your predominant psychological qualities are also reflected in your energetic self.

Everyone has had the experience of meeting someone who gives off a particularly powerful energy. The energy may be sexually seductive, or domineering, or feel fatherly or motherly. Alternatively, an individual may come across as seething with violence, or as being slippery and not to be trusted. What you are picking up is the quality of the person's energetic identity. A person's dominant energetic charge may be positive or negative, depending on what psychological qualities they have been fostering.

Of course, it is entirely possible to project your own feelings onto another person, such as motherly feelings onto a woman you wish to replace your own mother. So you may feel she has a motherly energy when she actually possesses nothing of the sort. Fear can also lead you to feel another is threatening when they are not. Projection is an issue whenever you seek to evaluate another on their own terms and not as an extension of your own feelings. Nonetheless, individuals certainly generate an energetic presence that others, when they are in a sufficiently sensitive state, feel strongly.

When a negative emotion is powerfully present in an individual's psychology over a period of time it gets transferred to the energetic self. This negative energy can then have a deleterious impact on the individual's physical, emotional and mental well-being. Physical illness is a common result. Where the illness attacks depends on the body's state. Usually, if a particular organ is already weakened due to previous experience, the negative energy will migrate to that weakened organ and illness results. Extended illnesses may result from sustained negative energies. Cancers are certainly generated as a result of sustained negative energy, although this is not so in all cases. Environmental impacts also cause cancers, which grow when an immune system is depleted, when small insults to the system repeatedly occur, or, in the case of exposure to radiation, when the body's natural defense system is simply blasted away.

Individuals also have a significant impact on their own health. Just as you can think yourself sick by repeatedly soaking yourself in negative images, feelings and ideas, so you can think yourself better by saturating yourself in positive images, feelings and concepts. This brings us back to the role of creative imagination.

Everyone's energetic self is impacted by their creative imagination. When you dwell on either positive or negative life scenarios you use your imagination. After repeatedly running related scenarios internally, those scenarios start manifesting in your behaviour. Athletes use their creative imagination in this way to maximise their performance in competition. Sprinters visualise how they will burst out of the blocks, what they need to do to accelerate to maximum speed, how they will place their feet, move their arms, and how they will manage the middle and end of the sprint. They visualise themselves doing what they have practised, reinforce to themselves that they are in great shape and are confident, and then strive to perform in competition all they creatively imagined during training.

Everyone does the same with their life. They creatively imagine what they will do. Then they act it out. If negative energy dominates an individual's psyche, then their selected scenarios will be negative and limiting rather than positive and growth oriented. Often people aren't consciously aware of the scenarios they are running in their head. They don't appreciate the degree to which their inner life revolves around limiting emotions, attitudes and thoughts, and how much those are tainting their outlook and behaviour. They especially aren't aware of how those negativities are creating negative energy at the level of their energetic self.

This is why adopting a self-analytical approach to your life is so important to living a satisfying life. It is doubly important if you wish to progress your spiritual understanding. If you are working to develop your sensitivity to subtle energies, then you need to purify the field of your energetic self, otherwise you will become attractive to identities you don't wish to encounter.

We have pointed out that the most common result of intense negative energy being present for an extended period is, first, emotional and psychological imbalance, then physical illness. Neither are pleasant or desirable. But they are not intrinsically different from a parasite being energetically attached to you. After all, viruses and bacteria are also parasites. They attach themselves to a part of the body and start eating. They reproduce, and collectively eat more and more, stressing the body, which leads to illness. Negative emotions similarly eat away at people, diminishing their psychological well-being and reducing their social functionality.

Looked at objectively, deeply embedded negative emotions and long-working bacteria and viruses are scarier than a spiritual identity that energetically attaches itself to you. This is because the energetic identity is relatively straight forward to get rid of—provided, of course, you know it is there. In contrast, deeply embedded emotions develop over years, and it usually takes some time to identify all the ways they influence you, decide on counter psychological strategies, and work to replace them with positive traits. Similarly, long-working viruses and bacteria can take an extended period to treat and for the body to recover its previous health.

The key in all three cases is diagnosis. You can't cure what you don't know about. And you can't understand all that is involved without appreciating your own psychological makeup and what particular traits led to whatever debilitating situation you are now in. This brings us to the other parts of the question you have asked.

What is the nature of these parasitical entities? Parasites exist within all strata of life. Everything physical feeds on something else. Numerous food chains exist on Earth, by which various creatures eat one another in order to live. Human beings take that one step further by growing other creatures specifically for food. Humanity envisions itself as being at the top of the food chain, which is why the idea that you in turn may be eaten is so distasteful to you. It contradicts your human self-image of being at the top of all food chains. Actually, each human body is eaten at the microbial level throughout its life. In this sense, energetic parasites are merely another form of what naturally exists in this planet's biosphere. They have as much right to live as viruses, bacteria or fungus spore that feed on trees and leaves.

Cling-ons and pick-ups are different forms of energetic parasites. Cling-ons, as the name suggests, are identities that perceive a food source and attach themselves to a creature's energetic envelope. In the physical world, some kinds of bacteria exist in symbiotic relationship to other species. For example, bacteria that live in the lining of cow's stomachs help transform grass into milk. Those bacteria don't live in other species' stomachs. Similarly, particular energetic parasites feed on particular species. The type of energetic identity that is attracted to you wouldn't be attracted to, say, a mouse, which manifests a different kind of energy to the human.

Pick-ups behave differently to cling-ons. Cling-ons tend to attach themselves to a host until they are expelled or become satiated. They then detach themselves and start looking for another host. In contrast, pick-ups are capable of jumping straight from one host to another. This usually happens because they perceive a new potential host with a higher level of energy than is possessed by their current host, so they hop from one to the other. They do so expressly when the potential new host is in physical proximity to the current host.

The question asserts that parasitical identities are dangerous because they can cause changes in the hosts inner state, shifting them from rational to irrational, pushing them to commit crimes, or even driving them mad. We disagree. This is not the case. Certainly, just as a physical parasite can lower the body's energy levels and stress the immune system, so an energetic parasite can lower the host's energy levels, which in turn leads to psychological stress. However, if an individual subsequently suffers from mood swings, becomes irrational, commits crimes or goes mad, that it not the parasitical identity's doing. Those behaviours result from tendencies already present within the individual's psyche.

As we observed earlier, it is the state of your energetic self that creates a condition that is attractive to parasites in the first place. This applies to both physical and energetic parasites. Physically, negative energy creates weaknesses in the body's organs and immune system, towards which viruses and bacteria naturally gravitate. Similarly, particular energetic parasites gravitate towards particular forms of negative energy, because that is what they feed on. But they don't create the energy. It's already there. Then, when individuals become stressed and psychologically debilitated, they behave in accordance with the negative energies present within their energetic self. So each human being is the source of their mood swings, irrational behaviour, criminal acts or madness. The energetic parasite is just along for the ride.

We again acknowledge that this whole scenario regarding energetic parasites sounds creepy. And it is—to those unfamiliar with what happens within the human domain. But if you take a low-key approach, and face up to, diagnose and treat whatever is present, then it is merely another aspect of maintaining your health. Appreciating the reality also offers an opportunity to learn.

Our scribe himself several months ago discovered two identities were attached to him. He became aware of them because a persistent itchy rash appeared on his left upper arm, then a lesser rash on his right upper arm. The situation was that one parasite was more experienced and stronger, and was teaching the other what to do. Our scribe was alerted to their presence first via thoughts planted in his mind, then via a dream. He used his intent to easily dislodge the weaker identity, but the other took three extended meditation sessions to dislodge. In the process he learned to draw on the powerful energy that his spiritual self has available. This influx of spiritual level energy, which he used his creative imagination to direct towards the parasite, essentially burnt off the interloper, much like a doctor burns a wart off the skin. The final phase is to use creative visualisation to heal the two places in his energetic envelope to which the parasites attached themselves. All this is part of learning about the relationship of the physical to the spiritual, and that the spiritual isn't distant. It is right here, right beside you and within you. And the energetic domain is the link between the two.

We conclude by answering the question regarding whether energetic parasites can interfere with or divert an individual's life plan. Individuals rarely include encountering energetic parasites in their life plan. Usually, they are just something that comes along during the natural course of experiencing life. On the other hand, guides may direct individuals towards such identities as part of their training, just as a doctor investigates bacteria as part of medical training. These identities cannot change a life plan. They are not that strong. If an individual has been diverted, it is because they choose to be diverted, or because a build-up of negative emotions and energy unbalanced their psyche sufficiently that they departed from what they intended to do.

As we have made clear, there is nothing intrinsically wrong in this. One opportunity is missed, but another opportunity replaces it. Being diverted from their life plan happens to everyone at some time, perhaps even many times. That is just part of experiencing life in the human world.

Question 15

Does praying do any good?

How about prayer? Do messages and feelings we send to those we love actually arrive? What about when we send a general prayer to express gratitude, to offer thanks, or to pray for the good of the world? Do these prayers arrive anywhere? Do they do any good?

THE GUIDES RESPOND:

This is a deep question that contains many facets. We'll start by discussing the nature of prayer. Prayer uses focused electromagnetic energy. Electromagnetic energy is central to the functioning of your brain and central nervous system. Sparks of electricity fire neurons so they can transfer information from one cell to another and stimulate hormones to send messages that regulate organs and bodily functions.

Prayers are messages that similarly consist of electromagnetic energy. When you pray, you focus your intent to create an emotional or intellectual message that is electromagnetic in nature. However, the difference between a prayer and what happens in your brain is that your brain's electromagnetic pulses are strictly local, being limited to your body's boundaries. In contrast, prayers are non-local communications, created specifically to be projected beyond the body, out into the world. Accordingly, we assert that prayers are really existing things. So where do they go?

The world is filled with all kinds of electromagnetic information: television and radio waves, microwaves for transmitting phone calls and SMS messages, x-rays, photons, and sub-atomic particles of all kinds—the list goes on. A prayer can be said to be just one among billions of electromagnetic signals passing across and through the surface of this planet. However, where some signals exist at the electrophysical end of the electromagnetic spectrum, others exist at the electrospiritual end of the spectrum. This means that machines such as radios, televisions and phones can pick up signals at the electrophysical end of the spectrum, but not signals at the electrospiritual end. These latter, which include prayers, are what may best be called mental in nature. The mental is not accessible to a physical apparatus. A mentally tuned apparatus is required, such as a mind, whether that mind is embodied or not.

Another basic difference between electromagnetic signals such as television signals and prayers is that the first category is transitory, whereas the second is not. By this we mean that a television signal is a package of information that exists as a wave that travels past a stationary receiver, such as a television antenna. When the television signal wave passes the antenna, it is gone and so is no longer accessible at that location. In contrast, a prayer is a packet of information that, once it is generated, continues to exist. It may be sampled by anyone who tunes into it, whatever their location, at any time.

What makes this possible is that prayers enter a holding station, a message database, if you will. This is an energetic repository that exists at a similar level to the cultural streams we have previously discussed. Like cultural streams, the repository for prayers contains information that exists at the electrospiritual end of the electromagnetic spectrum, and so can only be accessed by the minds of enquiring and sufficiently open spiritual identities.

The question arises that if a prayer is held in a huge database containing all the world's prayers, how does a prayer reach the particular person to whom it is addressed? There are two answers. To begin, it must be acknowledged that many prayers do not reach their intended recipients because the recipients aren't open to them, due to being insufficiently sensitive, or because they are sustaining animosity towards the sender, or simply because they aren't aware that such messages are available to be sipped.

We use the word *sipped* advisedly, because when you connect with the prayer repository and access a prayer directed your way, it is like sipping a refreshing or delicious drink. This is what results when the intended energy is transferred. Many people have had the experience of unexpectedly but delightfully receiving, in a quiet moment, a wash of a happy memory or love that appears to arrive out of nowhere. Sometimes the wave carries a memory of a specific person, usually the sender. But often the sender is not associated with the feeling, which conveys a general message of warmth and being cared for. This is the experience of a prayer being received.

On occasion someone else may intervene to help pass on a message or prayer. This is required because among people today there is a general lack of awareness regarding humanity's energetic possibilities, which results in few being trained in sending and receiving energetic messages. What happens is not so much that someone else actually passes on the message, but rather that they attract the recipient's attention and open him or her up to receiving the message, usually by planting a thought, an image or a dream in the recipient's mind. The recipient then remembers the sender, or perhaps a relevant past situation. Either opens them up sufficiently that they are able to receive the message. The recipient's spiritual self often stimulates and opens up the recipient's awareness in this way. However, soul friends and mentors may also perform that task, especially when it is important that an individual receive the message, but the intended recipient is proving particularly difficult to open up sufficiently to receive it.

We note that what we are describing here applies to messages of all kinds, not just prayers, prayers being a specialised form of messaging. Prayer is a specialised form of messaging because it involves faith. Faith needs to be briefly discussed due to its historical association with prayer. Among the religious, prayer is seen as an expression of faith. Believers have faith in God and in key spiritual figures of their religion, such as saints. They use prayers to petition these figures to intervene in the life (or afterlife) of a loved one. Such expressions of faith have their foundations in intensely felt emotion.

It could be said that a package of intention powers any prayer—we are referring to prayers that are stated with purpose and meaning and are not just repeated by rote. Christian theologians have teased out the intention that powers prayers into the separate strands of faith, hope and love. This quite successfully elucidates what is involved. Faith incorporates hope, because anyone who prays for another hopes to change their current and future life for the better. Prayers naturally contain love, because it is out of love that the sender intends any charitable act, including that of praying for another. Accordingly, we use the word *faith* here with the understanding that it actually consists of bundled faith-hope-love.

Note that people often use the word faith abstractly, in relation to a religious belief system. So it is common to refer to the Christian faith, the Buddhist faith, the Jewish faith, and so on. This is not how we are using the word faith here. Our understanding is that faith is primarily an intense emotion, being an intention manifested by a human individual to acknowledge, send support to, or energetically aid another. Faith may also be directed towards humanity as a whole, to sections of humanity, to other living creatures and species, or to the planet's biosphere. To sum up: when you send a prayer to someone, it is an act of faith sent in hope and motivated by love.

Some prayers are much stronger than others. When a group of people gather to send a supportive prayer to another, it is filled with the intent of all who are sending it. This certainly makes it a message worth receiving. How does a prayer arrive at the intended receiver? Through energetic signatures.

All identities have their own individual energetic signature. This applies whether they are in an embodied or a non-embodied state. In an embodied state, human identities have a layered signature, which consists of a blend of their biological, socialised, higher human, energetic and spiritual self's frequencies. In a non-embodied state, human identities have a pure spiritual level frequency. An individual's spiritual energetic signature changes as they evolve. Nonetheless, they always possess a unique signifier that identifies them as them and separates them from all other identities.

When a prayer is directed towards an individual it contains two energetic signatures, that of the sender and that of the receipient. If a group is sending the prayer, a collective signature is attached. These signatures are embedded energetically, through intention. Because senders initiate the prayer and sent it out, it automatically includes their energetic signature. Because senders use creative imagination to picture the intended recipient, the recipient's energetic signature is also tagged to the message.

How does the prayer arrive at the intended destination, given it enters an electromagnetic repository filled with billions of prayers? We can explain the process via the everyday example of a telephone call. A telephone call begins with the number being dialled. This ensures that among all the billions of calls being sent at the same time, the call is directed towards one particular telephone. The energetic signature tagged to a prayer is an identifier that may be likened to a telephone number. The identifier ensures the prayer arrives at the intended recipient. This is an overly crude analogy, but does reflect what happens. Of course, the recipient needs to *pick up* for the message to be received. We have already discussed this aspect of messaging.

As for general prayers that are not sent to particular individuals but rather to groups of people, or even to all humanity, these prayers go into what may be likened to an electromagnetic storage facility, which is filled with human-generated good intention. Much like a food warehouse, this repository of good intention is available to be drawn on when and as needed. This likely sounds somewhat nebulous and New Agey to you. However, we assure you that faith-filled prayers contribute to the repository of good intentions. It not only actually exists, but is needed to balance the greed, violence, and other forms of negativity perpetually generated by human beings. As such, it needs to be taken seriously and its purpose understood.

Today's scientists work on the assumption that everything consists of energy. The physical universe is a coagulation of energy in a particular range of frequencies. Microwaves are a coagulation at a different frequency range. Photons and muons are energy coagulated at sub-atomic frequencies. We agree with this scientific perspective. That is why we have characterised reality as being divided into the three broad bands of electrophysical, electromagnetic and electrospiritual energy, with a wide range of frequencies existing within each band.

You, as a spiritual identity, are a coagulation of electrospiritual energy. When you associate with a body for the term of a life, you are aligning your electrospiritual energy with a body's electrophysical energy. You use the body's associated network of electromagnetic energy to anchor yourself to the physical domain and to send messages between the electropsiritual and the electrophsyical bands.

One consequence of possessing an electromagnetic band of energy is that whatever a human being does has an energetic counterpart. This means acts of violence, exploitation or oppression generate not just a physical outcome but also an energetic outcome. This energetic outcome is a vibration that is added to the many other electromagnetic frequencies that surround this planet. From a spiritual perspective, the negative frequencies resemble a grey fog surrounding the Earth. This is psychologically unhealthy for human beings because it is as if everyone is perpetually living in and breathing poisonous smog. If you make no effort to change your energetic intake, you automatically inhale these human-generated negative energies. This is why negativity is so prevalent—and why those who do not become self-critically aware lapse into negativity so easily. Effectively, it is in the air. Attempting to become more spiritual by engaging in spiritual practices like prayer and meditation is significant because it helps counterbalance all the human-generated negativity. So, to answer the question, yes, on both the personal and planetwide levels, prayer is useful. It may be listed among the goods of human existence.

Becoming spiritual involves learning about the electromagnetic spectrum. You already utilise that spectrum automatically and unconsciously, because it enables you to exist as an fusion of spiritual intent and physical activity. Becoming spiritual involves learning to utilise the electromagnetic spectrum consciously and deliberately. That is why this question about prayer is important. It has enabled us to illuminate something of what is happening around you and to you, each moment of your life.

The electromagnetic spectrum sustains you. It provides nutrition, both physically, as in the television, phone and internet signals that keep modern civilisation functioning, and spiritually, in the form of subtle messages that provide you with important information and feed you with faith, hope and love. Adding to that, generating your own prayers is no more or less than an act of gratitude, via which you acknowledge the spiritual domain that sustains you and reciprocate with deep input of your own. Collectively, it provides spiritual nutrition for all who wish to imbibe it.

Question 16

Why is intention important?

You've repeatedly mentioned intention. What do you mean by intention? What is its significance to life in general and to meditation in particular?

THE GUIDES RESPOND:

Intention is fundamental to your existence. Whatever you think, say or do is a manifestation of your intention. Your intention drives you. What experiences you undergo, how you process your experiences, and what you decide to do next, all occur as a result of your intention. Intention provides you with your fundamental impetus as an individual. To understand what intention is you need to understand both the role of intention for humanity as a whole, and the nature of your personal intention and how it directs your life.

To begin at the spiritual level, before you incarnated you appraised a number of possibilities then decided on a course of action this time round. So your life plan is a manifestation of your spiritual you's intention. When you incarnated you encountered a body that had its own biologically-shaped intentions, involving eating, reproducing and surviving. You also developed a socialised self, which is focused on social concerns such as establishing relationships, finding work, and seeking success and happiness. During your childhood and teenage years you faced many difficult situations. In response, you developed psychological coping mechanisms. This in turn led to the formation of your gloopy self, which you use to get through life's fraught collisions. The gloopy self's intentions are largely self-defensive in nature—given that attacking and dominating are defensive behaviours as much as denying, avoiding and pretending not so see. Consequently, your spiritual self's intention, as manifested in your life plan, has been bluntened by the competing intentions of your biological, socialised and gloopy selves. All this makes discerning what intentions drive you from one day to the next a complex task.

It could be said there are three categories of intention: positive, limiting and neutral. We define these in relation to your life plan. Positive intentions are those that assist the realisation of your life plan, limiting intentions are those that limit or divert your life plan, and neutral intentions are those that are just present and neither help nor hinder. Understanding where the many intentions that drive you sit in this scale provides one of the key facets of self-knowledge.

A basic issue is that people aren't aware of their own intentions. As a result, unconscious drives and desires determine their life. For example, your parents may have instilled in you a sense of privilege or of inferiority. Or perhaps they repeatedly told you that the world is at your feet or that you will never amount to anything. As you age, much of what you do reflects your acquiescence to this parental patterning of your behaviour. Alternatively, you may rebel against it and do the opposite. This may be deliberately and consciously done, or it could be acted out unconsciously. All this makes appreciating what drives you a completely necessary task. Without self-knowledge your own intentions will remain opaque to you, while what is most significant to you—your life plan—will remain unknown.

Understanding your own multiple intentions, how they align and why they clash, will increase your life satisfaction manyfold. It will enable you to identify why you are obsessed with certain things, and it will help you get through trying times—because you'll understand the purpose of the obstacles you face, and appreciate where they fit into your larger plan. This is intention as it plays out psychologically. We'll now discuss intention on the energetic level.

One aspect of meditation we haven't yet discussed is using it to ignite your energetic envelope. We suggest you take time now to silence your mind, centre your attention in your awareness, then extend your awareness until you sense the outer limits of the energetic envelope that surrounds your body. Next use your creative imagination and picture the outer limits of your energetic envelope switching on and radiating energy, much like a bulb radiates light when the switch is flicked. Such an exercise supports your energetic health. It also reminds you that you are not not just a body, that you extend electromagnetically beyond your body's limits.

Intention on the electromagnetic level is a subtle affair. Each physical, emotional and mental activity has an electromagnetic counterpart. That is because, as the exercise will have made clear to you, your human you is not limited to your body but energetically extends a distance from it. And just as you can physically reach out and interact with a nearby person or object, so you can energetically interact with anything in your near vicinity. This is yet another complex topic. We do not have the space here to explore all the nuances involved. For now we will limit ourselves to a few introductory remarks.

When you intend to do anything, an energetic component is involved. For example, let's say you intend to join a course to extend your skill set. First you use your creative imagination to picture all the potential beneficial outcomes for you, then you sign up and pay the course fee. In doing this you make yourself energetically open, so when you turn up on the first day of the course, basically you are laying out a welcome mat and inviting your tutors and co-participants to enter your energetic envelope. Your tutors and co-participants do the same, their intention to participate similarly opening up their energetic envelopes. This facilitates a mutual exchange not just of practical, emotional and intellecual information, but also energetic information. When you come away from the course feeling inspired, you have certainly been stimulated emotionally and intellectually. But you have also been added to energetically. This occurred because you opened yourself up. That is, your intention was to learn from the workshop, and that lead to a multi-leveled interaction, including the energetic.

To illuminate this process a little more, let's look at the situation from another perspective. Let's say that your boss at work has instructed you to attend the course, and let's say you don't like your boss and you can't see the point of attending. You do so grudgingly, under duress. So when you turn up for the course you have no intention of giving it your all. Physically you are there, but emotionally, intellectually and energetically you resist engaging. Your shields are up. At the end of the day you come away feeling that the whole exercise was indeed a waste of time, and that you are vindicated in expecting it to be so.

Both these outcomes, one positive and growth oriented, the other negative and limiting, reflect your intention. In each case you got from the course what you expected. The mechanism by which you obtained the expected outcome was your intention. Your intention generated the outcome. Or, to be more exact, your intention created the conditions that brought about the outcome.

But what if your intention had changed during the course? What if you turned up expecting the course to be to a waste of time, but then you found yourself engaging with what the tutor was offering? What if by the day's end you had changed your orientation completely, and you went home feeling you had learned much more than you expected. What happens in such a circumstance?

Most people would say that the tutor overcame your doubts and your inhibitions, through the strength of their material or by virtue of their personal charisma, or both, and that's what changed your view. Certainly, this will probably be part of what happened. But the tutor likely arrived at the course expecting some participants to resist what was being shared. So the tutor began not just intending to share, but with the intention of overcoming resistance to what was being shared. This intention manifested on the energetic level, as well as practically, emotionally and intellectually. In other words, the persuasion had an energetic component. So when you came away at the end of the day, you left carrying energy deliberately intended by the tutor. The tutor energetically contributed to your change in response.

Collective energy creation is a common phenomenon. When you attend a sports event collective energy is generated by everyone present. This process also applies at political rallies, theatre performances, concerts, in hospital emergency rooms, and in train carriages during the peak hour commute. People often comment on the atmosphere in such places, referring to the shared excitement, powerful emotions, stress or alienation. They usually explain those shared atmospheres using emotional, psychological or industrial terms. In fact, it is the energy that is collectively generated in such situations that is the single over-riding reason they all feel similarly. The energy is primary, emotion is secondary, while intellectual rationalisation of the experience is tertiary. Collectively generated energy provides the chief explanation for unified mass behaviour, when massed people chant, feel and think the same thing. They are united energetically. To be more precise, they are hooked up energetically. To explain how this occurs, we need to introduce the notion of energetic hooks.

As well as opening you up energetically, intention is also able to throw out energetic hooks that become embedded in other people's energetic envelopes. In a situation such as attending a political rally, those attending don't just open themselves up energetically, allowing themselves to be swept along, they also send out little energetic hooks that bring them together. Usually this interchange of hooks will occur with people you know who are also attending, but if you meet someone who is vehement and forceful, and they direct their attention at you, in doing so they may lodge an energetic hook in your envelope.

Such hooks are normally small and easily dissolved. So when rally participants wake the following morning, they'll remember what they experienced, but as they become busy with the day's activities their memory of the rally will lose intensity. The energetic hooks they carried home from the rally will still be present, but if they don't re-engage with their experience, the hooks will start to dissolve.

However, someone else may wake the morning after the rally and feel it was one of the most thrilling events in their life. They then run it repeatedly through their mind, discussing it with themselves or others, reviving the emotions and turning over the words they found so stimulating. What they think they are doing is using their memory to relive the experience. This is partly so. But they are also using their intention to grasp the energetic hooks embedded in their energetic envelope. Grasping the hooks reanimates the rally experience and makes it that much more vivid and real. Energetic discharges will do that.

However—and here's the fascinating consequence—directing your intention towards an energetic hook not only causes energy to flow from the hook into your awareness. The act of directing your intention also generates energy that feeds the hook, so it grows. If you sustain your intention a feedback loop is established, in which you derive pleasure from grasping the hook, which feeds you its energy, and your intention in turn feeds the hook, which grows. This process of mutual reinforcement by intention and energetic hook occurs in both positive situations and in negative, self-limiting situations.

Of course, rallies use crude sloganeering that rarely reflect all the nuances of what participants think about whatever they have rallied to support or question. So the rally participants' energetic engagement varies considerably. As a consequence, the number of energetic hooks they leave with may be many, few or none. In this situation, the reason hooks exist at all is that the rally's energetic atmosphere is generated collectively. So while an orator may articulate what everyone thinks and feels, he or she does not create the energetic hooks.

The hooks are created by everyone jointly. How many hooks each participant leaves with depends on the level of their engagement, which depends how intensely their intention was aligned with the collective energy. To put it colloquially, the more they're into what's happening, the more hooks they bring to the party, the more hooks they share with others, and the more hooks they leave with.

What we have said so far about energetic hooks has been a general introduction on the small group and collective levels. This is because it is simpler to understand how hooks work in the context of public events. However, the fact is that energetic hooks are more significant, and certainly more prevalent, on the interpersonal level.

Any two people who are in a relationship—whether a love or a hate relationship—each direct their intention towards the other. Their intention involves physical, emotional and intellectual engagement, and also, as we have been discussing, an energetic component. This last leads to their embedding energetic hooks in each other's energetic envelope. If they remain together after their love fades, they may have many reasons for doing so: to raise their children, to protect their lifestyle, or just because life is easier that way. One contributing factor is that their mutually generated hooks tie them on the energetic level. An example is provided by the case of women who feel trapped in an abusive marriage. The original emotional ties that brought the couple together are broken, but even when physical support is offered by a social agency so the woman no longer needs her husband's money to feed and shelter their children, the hooks each has embedded in the other's energetic envelope still binds them. This is a significant contributing factor to why, after women have been physically removed from the situation, they return to the abusive relationship. Certainly, psychological factors may bring them back, but energetic ties are more difficult to break.

People embedding energetic hooks in one another is extremely common. Hooks exist because they are intended. People naturally want to be loved, want to be wanted, want to be essential to another. Children are naturally dependent on their parents, and parents naturally want to protect and nurture their children. So the fact that people embed energetic hooks in each other is a natural part of their mutual engagement. It provides a way for those who love and care for each other to remain attached and in sync. And it all happens as a result of their aligned intentions and the many connections, including the energetic, that their intentions create.

One interesting consequence of this is that when the telephone rings and people know who is calling before they pick up, they assume they are being psychic. Actually, what happens is that the phoning person has formed an intention to communicate, and their intention has reached out and touched the hook embedded in the other's energetic envelope. It is that glowing hook, stimulated by the caller's intention, that enables the called person to know who is phoning.

This shows that energetic hooks are not a bad or negative thing. They are useful and positive. If you are emotionally or intellectually attuned to another, it is highly likely you are energetically hooked in and fuelling each other. Hooks are a valuable way of sustaining connection.

There *is* a downside to hooks, however. When a relationship ends, each person's hooks remain embedded in the other's energetic envelope. The hooks themselves are not a negative presence, although if the relationship involved negative psychological traits they will carry negative energy. Yet hooks that are no longer needed can be troublesome because for some people burying hooks in another involves a consciously or unconcsciously generated degree of wanting to control them. There is also the aspect of one person wanting others to be tied close and not wanting to let them get away.

When considering the terminology to describe this process, we could have selected *connection*, a neutral word. However, after reflection we decided *hook* was more appropriate, given electric wires and implements are said to be hooked up, and when two friends or lovers meet somewhere it is described as hooking up. Of course, the unacknowledged consequence of hooks is that you can get caught on them. It was this idea of getting caught that lead us to prefer *hook* over *connection*. At times energetic hooks are certainly created out of a coercive or controlling intention, with another being energetically hunted like a fish, hooked, and reeled in. Yet, as we have pointed out, most commonly hooks are generated out of a connective intention, as part of the exchange of deep feelings people have for one another.

So what do you do about another's energetic hooks that remain embedded in your energetic envelope, and yours in theirs', after the relationship has ended? Are they a problem? The short answer is: it depends. Sometimes they are. Mostly they aren't. They are a problem if the other person had intense feelings about you, or you about them, that you or they still carry, and especially if those feelings carry negative energy. Then you are certainly advised to dissolve them.

It is recommended that, to fully develop your energetic self's potential, it is useful to dissolve all the hooks left over from expired relationships, whether those relationships involved love, work or play. Accordingly, as a meditation exercise, we suggest you focus on your energetic envelope, energise it by drawing energy from your spiritual self via the belly button chakra, then use that energy to dissolve all those hooks you no longer require. We also suggest you call back and dissolve the hooks you have left in others who are long gone from your life. Intention created the hooks in the first place. You can now use intention to call them back and dissolve them.

Much else can and will be said about intention on the energetic level. However, this provides some introductory remarks on the nature of intention and how it plays out energetically.

Can we imbue objects or places with energy?

Can people intentionally create energetic darts to harm others? What about power objects? Can anything be filled with healing power or other kinds of energy? And can places be imbued with personal energy? I'm thinking of the ghosts of dead people who haunt houses or woods. Then there are saints who are said to have energised their tombs with spiritual power. Does this really happen? If so, what process is involved?

THE GUIDES RESPOND:

Much of what we discussed in the last response deals with energetic connections that exist at the subconscious level, which people intend without being fully aware of what is happening or what results. That is why we recommended you use meditation to become more conscious of your energetic footprint and the trail it is leaving in the world. This question shifts to a consideration of energetic activity that is deliberately and consciously intended. As such, it opens up useful territory that we are very happy to discuss.

Can people create energetic darts intended to harm others? Yes. Various shamanic traditions point to this very phenomenon. Of course, no one gets away with anything. Harming others generates negative karma that will need to be repaid. So creating energetic darts is not a recommended practice. What *is* recommended, in certain circumstances, is making an effort to imbue an object with energy. In practice, forming a harmful dart and imbuing an object with energy involve the same process, so we'll begin by describing what happens when an object is energetically imbued.

At this point our scribe asks, why would you fill an object with energy in the first place? In the past it was most often done to carry an intention across generations. The intention was usually to heal, to stimulate a search for knowledge, or to forge an energetic connection with the object's future owner. These kinds of power objects also had a symbolic shape, design or function that contained a message. This meant that the intent transmitted into the object added an energetic dimension to the message. In this way individuals used a statue, carved rock, or a pendant to pass their intent to later generations. Naturally, whoever received the object would need to tune themselves to the same energetic level to tap into what the object had to convey. This is a practice that was prevalent in ancient times, but has fallen away today.

We also observe that this practice is based on a false assumption. The person who energises an object is operating at the level of their embodied awareness. However, they could more effectively communicate with later generations in the non-embodied state undergone between lives. Then they will have many more resources at their disposal, including a significantly higher level of subtle energy to effect the desired result. It would also be more effective for the individual to work directly with whoever in later generations they wished to stimulate. This could be done by helping train that individual between lives, or by making an agreement to meet in a future life where they could exchange energy directly. On the other hand, the exercise of imbuing an object with personal energy has certainly helped many individuals appreciate the capacities of their energetic self.

Those who in earlier times sought to imbue an object to harm another had two strategies. One was to project their intention into a weapon or bauble the victim would pick up. The intention was that when the energised object made physical contact with the victim the harmful energy would pass to them. In this case the object functioned as an intermediary. The second strategem was for the one intending harm to do so mentally, using creative imagination to direct the energy.

Is there defence against such stratagems? There is. The first is to stay away from those who would do so. To achieve this you have to be alert and be able to psychologically read others. On the other hand, anyone who carries that degree of malevolence should not be difficult to spot. We add that this activity frequently occurred in the past in traditional tribal cultures, but is rare in the modern Western world. If someone today really wishes to pursue you, you can use the meditation practices we have described to transform your energetic envelope into a protective shield. You can also call on mentors and guides if you are seriously concerned. But, as we said, today this situation rarely occurs. Many people would go through their entire reincarnational cycle and be on neither the giving nor receiving end of such malevolence.

The question was asked whether the ghosts of deceased people haunt particular places? The answer is, yes. Why? Sometimes because they feel they have unfinished business, such as wanting their death to be acknowledged or avenged. Sometimes people get confused and don't realise they are dead, or they do realise it but don't know what to do next, so they hang around a familiar place and frustratedly try to attract the attention of the living. Sometimes spirits that haunt a place in a way that scares people, perhaps by rattling pots or slamming doors, are not deceased human beings at all, but are spiritual identities having a little fun. They are curious, like a teenager would be, and try things on for a while. A steady intent directed at them will send them on their way. Sometimes a deceased human being will create mischief. They also just require a steadily extended invitation to move on.

How a newly deceased individual remains earthbound is that they direct their intent towards a particular physical place, and that in-tention sustains their energetic connection with it, keeping them nearby. When most people find their body has died, they recognise what has happened, shift their intent to the electrospiritual, and disconnect from the physical realm quite quickly. However, there are always outliers who either leave their body before it has died, or hang around long after it has gone. Is anything wrong with either response? No. Each offers further opportunities for experience.

The question was asked if deceased saints can imbue a tomb with their spiritual vibration. They can. But why would anyone bother? Numerous opportunities are available in the multiverse and throughout all the spiritual regions that penetrate it. Very few of those regarded as saints have lived their final incarnation, so after their body dies they will be busy reviewing their just-completed life, organising the next one, and doing further training to prepare. They have too much going on to bother hanging around a grave all day.

In putting it this way we are being somewhat facetious. However, we do so to counteract the widespread human assumption that spirituality revolves around specific physical places on the Earth. It doesn't. Spiritual communication can and does occur anywhere, at any time, to anyone. No plugging into saints or holy places is required.

The reason so-called sacred and holy places exist—and many places certainly do have an intense energy centred on them—is that those in spirit make use of human assumptions, even those that are erroneous, and use places of pilgrimage to feed seekers energetically and spiritually. Religious worshippers who undertake pilgrimages open themselves up energetically and so become more available to receive the messages or experiences they require at that time. When an individual feels driven to visit a sacred place, those who are not merely fulfilling a social contract are usually driven by their own spiritual self. So when they arrive it is often their spiritual self, or a personal mentor or guide, who sends the message or experience. It may also be a spirit who is associating with the site for a time. The saint who is buried in the tomb is not involved, given he or she is usually long gone.

Non-embodied human beings also make use of sacred sites for their own between life training. They do it to develop the art of giving uplift and aid to those who require solutions to their life problems. In effect, energised sacred sites may be thought of portals that are served by a constantly changing cast of spiritual identities, each of whom is trained in spiritual care and has been assigned a period of duty.

As with haunted houses, sometimes non-human spirits visit such places, but this is rare. The usual procedure is that those who are vibrationally close to embodied humanity carry out this nurturing task—we refer in particular to those who are still living out their incarnational cycle, or who have recently finished their cycle and are working to help the incarnated while their soul companions finish their own cycles. As we have said before, those in the non-embodied domain are just as occupied as those who are embodied.

One other variety of spirit deserves mention here. These are what have historically been called nature spirits. These spirits associate with particular places, imbuing them with often extraordinary energy. They are non-human in nature and rarely associate with buildings, being naturally aligned to mountains, valleys, or woods. Why do so? For the same reason you incarnate in a body: to experience the physical domain, to interact, and to learn. They differ from you in that they do not live inside any species. Rather, they associate with a natural formation or growth like a wooded area, acting as its guardian. Every habitat has diverse flora and fauna for a guardian spirit to oversee and experience. Because nature spirits can associate with a place for thousands of years, they develop great depth of knowledge. Ancient tribal cultures regularly consulted these spirits, who advised them on what to cultivate and eat, and how to survive. Today the knowledge and respect required to facilitate such communication has fallen away. Nonetheless, sensitive people certainly notice the energy powerful nature spirits add to natural sites, to the degree that those places come to be called sacred.

Question 18

How do I use intention to explore imaginal realms?

You said we have multiple intentions swirling inside us, that they collide and work against each other. How can I be sure unconscious intentions aren't interfering when I meditate? How can I be sure my intention is correct, assuming there is such a thing?

THE GUIDES RESPOND:

Intention is the driver. Intention gets things done. If you say you intended to do something but you never got around to doing it, you are actually talking about wishes. A wish is a pre-formulation of an intention. A wish becomes an intention when you focus on it, instil it with energy, and enact it to achieve a particular goal.

We observed earlier that many intentions are unconsciously formed and activated. The gloopy self's defensive strategies, in which it attacks another when it feels threatened, or when it deflects or runs away, are behavioural patterns that were set in motion long ago, typically during childhood. They now operate on auto-pilot. They are examples of behaviour that is unconsciously intended.

Other intentions are more consciously shaped, but have a similar defensive purpose. Let's say, for example, that at your place of work you strategise to get a pay rise or promotion. That may require you to step on another's toes, or to be obsequious, or to falsely present your own or another's abilities. This type of crafty behaviour is deliberately and consciously intended. It is a manifestation of your gloopy self.

We mention these two kinds of gloopy intention because, when you cross the threshold and enter the imaginal realm, if you are motivated by unconscious or crafty intentions you will not do well. Purity of intention is required to forge an energetic and spiritual relationship with those you encounter.

Spiritual identities easily see when you are driven by gloopy intentions. It appears as a fog on your energetic envelope and adds discolouration to your communications. It is then up to the identity to decide whether or not it will ignore your gloop and communicate with you. If the identity doesn't know you, it will likely shy away. Only if you have already established a relationship is the identity likely to ignore the gloop. Just as you do when dealing with others you care for, it would rationalise that the gloop is a passing phase, which it hopes will be dispelled as the two of you come into alignment. Of course, there is also the possibility that an identity who enjoys human gloop will be attracted to you, to your possible discomfort.

This explains why so many interactions between human beings and spiritual identities involve a teaching relationship, with non-embodied spirits offering advice to the embodied. Most embodied individuals possess some gloopiness. They also go through periods when the level of their gloopy energy goes up and down. Spiritual identities most commonly look past the gloop and interact because (1) they perceive an individual's potential, (2) they recognise that a particular form of gloopiness is part of the incarnate individual's life plan, or (3) a wider intention is in play and an individual has a role to perform, being a small cog in a larger, probably unseen, wheel. It could be said that in such situations communication is sustained, and gloopiness is ignored, for the sake of the greater good.

The greater good operates on a number of levels. Your personal greater good consists of the evolving spiritual identity of which your current human self is a small contributing part. Your evolving spiritual identity, in turn, contributes to the greater good of the extensive entity of which it is a fragment. Physically and planetwide, the greater good involves the communities in which you live and the biosphere in which humanity exists. Humanity's greater good extends across generations, such as when people plant trees for the sake of those who will be born long after they are deceased, or when people create educational materials, such as this book, for others they don't know, whether they are currently living or yet to be born. All these are aspects of what we mean by the phrase *the greater good*.

We introduce this idea here because when you initiate a journey into the imaginal realm, and when you seek information or help from those existing there, it is useful to keep in mind that what you are doing is for the greater good—your own, because you are aiding your personal growth, and others', given that what you find will be shared. Keeping in mind your endeavours are for the greater good will help ensure that your intentions remain pure. Saying a small prayer before you begin meditating both helps focus your mind and reminds you to positively align your intention. Sustaining a sense of your smallness in relation to what you usually think of as being greater than you is also useful.

But don't confuse this intent with being insignificant. Don't think that, given the vastness of what is, whatever you do doesn't matter. That is your gloopy self talking. The fact is that if a machine lacks a small cog it won't work. Similarly, everyone, no matter how big or small, is a cog in a larger wheel. There is always someone who is more able than you, and someone else who doesn't know and can't do what you know and can do. So remember that whatever you bring back from the imaginal realm is not only significant to you, it will also be useful to those you share it with. It contributes to the greater good.

If you establish this mindset, we assure you your intentions will always be correctly aligned and your meditation practice will produce sound outcomes.

Question 19

So where *do* I go
when I meditate?

What happens when I meditate? If I'm entering the imaginal realm, where does my mind go? I ask because when I mediate I'm still aware of my body. Does this mean my mind is in two places at once? Or does my mind split into two? What actually takes place? What happens and where do I go?

THE GUIDES RESPOND:

We could answer the question of where do you go when you meditate by using enigmatic Zen terminology and say that you don't go anywhere, that you're already there. However, while this is true, it only half explains what happens when you meditate.

To use a term currently in vogue in spiritual circles, reality is multi-dimensional. Our interpretation of this word is that different levels of reality are present simultaneously, interpenetrating each other. However, you only become aware of these layers by changing your mode of perception. Changing your mode of perception in turn relies on raising your energy, as a result of which you enter a heightened state of awareness. This way you perceive what you previously haven't. The simple analogy of changing glasses explains the process.

When you wear rose-tinted glasses you see the world around you as rosy, because the lenses filter out the green portion of the light spectrum, accentuating the red. In ordinary states of awareness, the human brain acts as just such a filter, allowing in only a limited range of the electromagnetic spectrum, filtering out much. Just as rose-tinted glasses provide a rosy view of the world, so the human brain's cognitive capacities provide a human view of reality. When you enter a heightened state of awareness, in effect you change glasses. Your brain's normal perceptual processes are replaced by a new mode of perception.

This, then, is a simple way of explaining what happens when you meditate: you enter a heightened state of awareness, which results in you changing glasses (adopting a new mode of perception), and so you perceive aspects of reality you previously haven't. However, as you no doubt will expect of us by now, we add that actually the situation is not quite this straightforward. This is because while meditating you don't really change one set of glasses for another. Rather, you wear two sets of glasses simultaneously. We'll explain.

When you meditate, you still your thoughts, focus your intent, and eventually enter a heightened state of awareness. At this point you activate a second level of awareness, centred in your spiritual self. So you now have one level of awareness, your everyday level, which is centred in your everyday mind, and you have a second level of awareness, centred in your spiritual self's mind. The result is that you can simultaneously be aware of where your body is, let's say seated in a room in your favoured meditation posture, and also be aware that you are receiving non-physical perceptions. Your awareness is simultaneously locally situated, in your body, and non-locally situated, in the imaginal realm.

So when you meditate, your body remains in the physical world, and the corresponding aspect of your awareness remains locally situated. In that case, where is the non-locally situated aspect of your awareness? Where does it go? We just said your awareness enters the imaginal realm. But where is that? And how is it structured? We have already partly answered this question in Question 9. Feel free to review it. However, we will now add a little more to what we said there.

Throughout the ages, the imaginal realm has been defined in many ways by different religions and spiritual traditions. Definitions vary from the simple Christian idea that the imaginal realm consists of heaven, purgatory and hell, to the more sophisticated shamanic division of reality into the lower, middle and upper worlds, to the complex Theosophical division of the astral, mental, buddhic, and so on.

Undoubtedly, a map is useful when you visit a city that is new to you. Similarly, it is useful having some idea of how to locate yourself when your awareness enters the imaginal realm. However, we recommend that you keep your mind as fresh as possible when you first do so. This is so you don't perceive what you experience through a pre-ground lens. It is much preferable you not try to fit your perceptions into pre-formulated schemata. Instead, we suggest you maintain an empirical approach. That is, put your emphasis on your actual perceptions, and only attempt to categorise or explain them after you have accumulated a sufficient volume of data to warrant doing so.

Jumping to conclusions regarding your perceptions is never recommended, especially after just one or two experiences. Neither do we recommend journeying with ready-made notions of what may happen. Doing so will limit your perceptions, because they effectively become glasses that filter what you experience. Only after you have had a considerable number of experiences are you in a position to start generating a map of the territory you have uncovered. Even then you will only have experienced a tiny portion of multi-dimensional reality.

Of course, this doesn't preclude you initiating a meditation session for the purpose of asking a particular question or seeking specific knowledge. Certainly shape an intent and hold to it. But don't second-guess answers. Form your intent, then remain as open as you can. Only then can you be assured that what you perceive is not a projection of either what you desire or what you already know. Even then, still question your perceptions. Remain sceptical in a positive way. And remember, there is always more to learn.

Regarding what levels of multi-dimensional reality you may potentially access, we will make no firm statements. As we have previously said in relation to forging pathways into the *jungle*, individuals have their own interests, their own issues to resolve, and their own prior experiences. This naturally leads them to explore one aspect of the spiritual realm rather than others. One person becomes an expert medium, focussing on communications with non-embodied identities, while another develops expertise in other forms of communication. You can only follow your own course, pursuing what interests you and what satisfies your current concerns.

From an experiential perspective, that fact that your awareness remains connected to your body means that even if you travel a long way, which some of those who master out-of-body travel do, you will always retain a dual awareness. This is so even when you lose all awareness of your body, which every meditator does at some time, because an energetic cord still connects your awareness to your body, bringing you back the moment something disturbs it. Only between lives, when you have no body, do you have greater freedom to travel through multi-dimensional reality. Yet even then you can only access realms you energetically vibrate in sympathy with, whether at your own or a lower level. Higher vibrating realms will remain inaccessible until you raise your vibration to a level sufficient to perceive them.

So, to return to our opening statement, while reality is multi-dimensional, with many levels of reality existing around you and inter-penetrating you, you can only currently access a miniscule portion of it. How far you penetrate into the spiritual realm, and what kinds of experiences you have, depend on you, your interests, what practices you take up, and how intensely you apply yourself.

Question 20

Is all of me here?

Some people claim that not all their spiritual self is present in their body. They offer two explanations. One is that the human body is not vibrationally strong enough to hold all of our spiritual self, that our spiritual energy is too great. The other is that while we are embodied part of us is doing other things, beyond the human. Is that happening? Is all of me here?

THE GUIDES RESPOND:

This is another topic that has generated confusion, chiefly because, like much else regarding human existence, what is involved is multi-faceted. Individual cases vary. Many permutations are possible in how the physical, energetic and spiritual elements of your current configuration interact. It is simply impossible to list all the possibilities here.

In saying this, we are aware of repeatedly stating in our answers that the human situation is complex, that no one-size-fits-all explanations are possible, and accordingly we can't fully satisfy enquiries into these matters. As a reader you may even feel we have asserted this ad nauseam. In response, we make the following points.

First, after you finish reading this series of responses, we want you to take away the certainty that there is a huge amount you don't know about your own awareness and what it is capable of doing. It is able to accomplish things that are simply inconceivable to you, given the degree to which all human beings' outlooks are conditioned and limited by the norms of everyday existence. We include in these norms aspects of religious and spiritual teachings passed down through the ages. While many valid notions sit at the heart of religious and spiritual traditions, in most cases they are overlaid by fantasy and dogma. We encourage you to shrug off these inherited notions and adopt what, in the previous response, we called an empirical outlook. Whatever non-everyday experiences and perceptions you have, address them directly, processing them on their own terms, without filtering them through adopted ideas. This, then, is our first point: accept that there is far more that you don't know than you do.

Second, keep exploring, keep questioning, keep digging into what lies behind your life circumstances. Keep investigating the layers of your own nature, as well as the layers of reality that surround you. Not only do we advise you not to accept easy answers, we propose that even when you uncover more extensive answers than you expected, which explain more than you had previously considered, don't stop there. Keep exploring. Keep questioning. Too many people reach a certain level of perception and understanding, consider it sufficient, and stop. It isn't sufficient. There is no need to stop. No perception is a complete perception, no understanding is the final understanding. So this is our second point: keep exploring, keep progressing.

Third, related to the second, is that no one has all the answers. We include ourselves in this. What we are attempting to do is make observations on the human situation that are fuller than what is now commonly understood, but that are not so expansive as to be incomprehensible. Our intention is to encourage you to move forwards, but without describing your next steps in ways that makes them appear too difficult. We don't want you to despairingly throw your hands in the air and not make an effort because it is all too hard. We want to challenge you, not puncture you. This, then, is our third point: our responses are working explanations. They are not the final word.

They are, to use a concept drawn from Zen Buddhism, fingers pointing towards the moon. You need fingers pointing, you need clarifying explanations, in order to know where you are and to appreciate how to move forwards. So ours are pragmatic statements, offered to guide you during your endeavours. They are like signs placed along the highway to indicate your next big tourist experience.

Fourth, you *are* a tourist. By taking on human incarnation you have signed up for a big adventure. One common notion of being a tourist is that it involves going on holiday to an exotic destination and there you lie on the beach or beside the hotel pool drinking pina coladas. This is not the notion of tourism we are proposing.

Another form of tourism involves travelling to a foreign place you haven't previously visited and immersing yourself in its culture. This is closer to what we mean, because descending from the spiritual domain into a human body often involves you in situations you have not previously experienced. However, the fact is that human incarnation can be more fraught than this suggests, given it usually involves difficult situations, thwarted intents, and impossible people. To continue the analogy, incarnating is like being a tourist in a foreign country, but finding your bags have been stolen, your hotel booking misplaced, and you really don't like the food.

This brings us to a third variety of tourism, extreme adventure tourism, which involves tourists challenging themselves to climb mountains, paddle dangerous rivers, and strap themselves into wings before throwing themselves off cliff tops. This much more accurately reflects what human incarnation is like, and is closer to what we intend by describing you as a tourist. So human existence may be likened to extreme adventure tourism.

This brings us to our final point about being a tourist. Business and the military share a notion that individuals go on a tour of duty. A tour of duty involves travelling to a foreign country for the purpose of carrying out a specific task. The tour lasts until the task is completed.

This definitely also accords with our idea of being a tourist. You have incarnated to do a tour of duty. However, you likely have several tasks to complete, not just one, and numerous difficulties are almost certain to be involved.

Our notion of tourism combines all these concepts. By incarnating you have travelled to the equivalent of a foreign country, are experiencing a new culture, have a number of tasks to complete, and sometimes you feel you've been thrown off the top of a cliff. All this makes you an extreme adventure tourist who has undertaken a tour of duty in a foreign country.

Fifth, we observe that *you* are the tourist. *You* are the one who experiencing the tour of duty. *You* are the one who has to go through what happens, however it turns out. *You* are the one who is experiencing and learning. No one else can go through the adventure for you. No one else can learn on your behalf. You have to do it all.

So when you get into an extreme situation, it is *your* extreme situation. You got yourself into it, you selected it—whether consciously or unconsciously—and you're the one who has to get through and reach the other side. If you're in a canoe on a rough river, no one else is going to step in and magically lift you out, even though you may feel you're in over your head. You have to use your own ingenuity to get through the rapids and reach calm water.

Of course, when you embark on an extreme river trek, if your canoe tips up guides are there to stop you drowning. Similarly, you have friends in spirit who are looking out for you. But there's no point them stepping in merely when you start to panic. That would defeat the whole point of going on an extreme adventure. You've chosen that particular trip because you wish to challenge yourself. You are learning through doing. So everyone in spirit lets you get on with it—with the one caveat that if you're really headed in the wrong direction, or if your head is repeatedly going under water, your friends in spirit will give you a supportive push or pull to get you back on track.

To summarise our fifth point: it's up to you. You're doing it. And if you don't, no one else will step in and do it for you. Dawdle in this life and you'll just have to set up a similar tour of duty and do it all over again. There's no escaping this process. So our advice is to make the most of whatever presents itself and energetically throw yourself into it.

All this is a very long introduction to answering the question. However, it is necessary because it leads into several observations we wish to make regarding whether all of you is here.

To begin, we agree that, yes, not all of your spiritual you, by which we mean your full identity at the spiritual level, is present within your current human personality. We have previously offered a model in which the self consists of five layers we labelled selves: the biological self, the socially formed self, the higher human self, the energetic self, and the spiritual self. In response to the question, we can say that the spiritual self, which is buried deep within you, consists of only a portion of your full spiritual identity. What size portion? In general, somewhere between 20% and 80%. Why such a difference? This is where individual cases need to be taken into consideration.

Let's say you have had a series of tough lives, in which you previously went through some difficult situations. Alternatively, you may be in a tender state internally, and to rebuild your confidence you need to take it easy for a period. In each case, what is needed is a minimally stressful life. For the first person, who has previously had to deal with tough situations, low stress helps the absorption of tough life lessons. For the second, who for whatever reason is inwardly tender, a low stress life gives them time to get their breath back, so to speak, to regather their wits and enthusiasm. In these two cases an undemanding life is selected, involving minimal problems. The individuals concerned may decide they only need to utilise 20% or 30% of their full spiritual identity. So they send down only this percentage of their total spiritual presence to make up the spiritual self component of their five-layered incarnated self.

Alternatively, someone who has booked a tough tour of duty for themselves, involving extreme encounters, may choose to send down 50% or 60% of themselves. This because they expect to be severely tested and want to be able to draw directly on their prior experience so they can successfully deal with the demands.

Do people sometimes send down too little or too much of their spiritual identity to constitute their human embodied spiritual self? Yes. What happens then? In the case of too little presence in difficult situations, individuals may end up getting overwhelmed and not be up to doing what they planned. It is like being on holiday in a foreign country, thinking you don't need to learn the language to communicate, then arriving, finding no one speaks your language, and suddenly you don't know what's going on or what you are supposed to do next. The experience rapidly gets much more difficult than you planned.

In the case of someone who sends too much of their full spiritual identity into the spiritual self that underpins their personality, they may end up not being challenged as much as they intended, and so don't test parts of themselves in the ways they planned. They may even end up feeling somewhat bored. Why?

At the level of your spiritual self you possess a great deal of experience and knowledge. Having access to more of this store means your human you is able to come up with work-arounds when faced with awkward situations. So rather than going into a problem, working through it, and coming out the other side feeling more experienced and wiser, you instead have the savvy to sidestep the problem and work around it. To keep our tourist metaphor going, it is like travelling to a foreign country and having a translator/manager on tap who has seen all your problems before so solves them without your current personality needing to really come to grips with them. This is unsatisfactory because it results in your learning much less than you intended when you originally planned the life.

How do you decide how much of your spiritual vibration you

should send down to form the spiritual self deep within each personality? Initially, individuals are given advice. But once they reach the teen part of their incarnational cycle, the decision is left to them. Their experience then becomes their guide. Can individuals overestimate their capability? Certainly. Do they do so repeatedly? No. Doing so messes up their tour and becomes counterproductive. The art of incarnating involves learning to balance the difficulty of the challenges you line up for yourself with the psycho-spiritual resources you select for that life—because you don't just select a certain percentage of spiritual presence, you also select a range of positive and limiting psychological traits, all of which you draw on to grapple with life situations. Different lives present different problems so require different resources. That is why we say no one-size-fits-all formula suits all lives.

Does anyone send 100% of their spiritual presence into the spiritual self portion of the five-layered human self? No. Why not? Several factors account for this. One is that, as the question observed, the human body's nervous system isn't capable of energetically containing all your spiritual you. The two vibrations exist on very different levels, with the physical body being on a much coarser, cruder level than your spiritual part. This disparity becomes even greater as your spiritual identity evolves.

When you begin your incarnational cycle your spiritual identity is inexperienced. It has limited personal resources. By the time you have undergone a thousand incarnations, when you are reaching the end of your cycle, this situation has changed considerably. You are more experienced, you have developed numerous abilities, you know intimately how the human domain functions, and you can calmly cope with anything human life throws at you. You are innately more knowing and more loving. You have become wise.

The upshot of this is that, as a general rule, it may be said that inexperienced individuals put more of their spiritual presence into their incarnated human self, and experienced individuals put in less, simply because, energetically speaking, experienced individuals have evolved into a much greater spiritual presence, and less and less of it is able to fit into a human awareness.

To offer a final observation on this issue of proportion, we would say that the balance between the percentage of spiritual presence you inject into your incarnated self and the percentage you choose to remain in a non-embodied state also impacts of the degree to which you feel grounded in your human identity. By *grounded* we mean spiritually grounded.

For example, when an individual first starts their incarnation cycle, if they send 70% of their spiritual presence into their incarnated self, and due to inexperience feel overwhelmed by their life circumstances, their spiritual self, which is buried down within them, is also overwhelmed. The result is that because a high percentage of their spiritual presence is present in their human self, yet is inaccessible, they would likely feel highly destabilised. That is, they would have little non-embodied spiritual presence to call on, and that little is inexperienced and so unable to help much even if it could come to their aid. But if the same individual sent just 20% of their spiritual presence to live that same life, then they retain 80% of their spiritual presence to provide support and soothing assistance from outside their incarnated self. In such a case, the non-embodied 80% is better able to help the embodied 20% cope than the non-embodied 30% is able to help the embodied 70% cope. This is simplistic maths, but it offers a reasonable account for why an inexperienced identity normally sends a lesser percentage of its overall vibration into a body.

In contrast, a very experienced individual may choose to send 60% of their spiritual presence into their incarnated self, because they have developed the skill to access the resources of their embodied spiritual self. Calling on those inner resources is likely to be part of how they are testing themselves in that life. On the other hand, an equally experienced individual may choose to send down only 40%, because they are working on establishing a bridge between their human awareness and their spiritual identity and want to have a high percentage of their non-embodied spiritual self available to call on. As can be seen, there are many reasons why no one sends all of their spiritual presence into a body.

To summarise, no human bodies, as they are currently constituted, are able to contain all the energy of your spiritual presence. On the other hand, given the limitations of the human cognitive system, why would anyone want to? If they sent a high percentage of their spiritual presence into a body, much of it would remain underutilised. To depict the situation light-heartedly, your spiritual you would be seated inside your human you, twiddling its thumbs. The situation would be a waste of your deepest resources.

What does that non-incarnated portion of your spiritual identity get up to when you are living your human life? A portion is directed towards you, offering support, aid and advice in the ways we have previously outlined. A larger or smaller portion of your spiritual identity will be involved in this support, depending on what you are doing in your life and how much you have planned to actively involve your non-embodied identity this time round. For example, someone devoted to spiritual practice is likely to involve more of their non-embodied identity than another person who is focused entirely on their physical or psychological accomplishments. We don't say this to disparage physical and psychological accomplishments, just to point out that in general they don't require as much active input from your non-embodied resources. The requirements are different so different resources are directed at them. It is an example, as the adage goes, of different strokes for different folks.

While you are embodied, is your spiritual identity doing things that have nothing to do with your current life? Sometimes. This is likely to occur more with an experienced individual than one who is inexperienced, basically because the experienced have developed more personal resources, which they can simultaneously direct into a life and beyond that life. What sort of things? Often your non-embodied portion will be focused on the same issues you are, but from the other end of the stick, so to speak. For example, while you are learning to meditate, your non-embodied portion will be learning related skills, including how to better communicate with your human you. This involves learning to pass on information via dreams and during the heightened states of awareness you enter while meditating. For you in a human body, skill-building involves directing your awareness up into the spiritual realm, while on the spiritual level it involves learning to communicate down, into your human you. Note that *up* and *down* are metaphors, because the physical and spiritual exist in parallel, inter-penetrating one another. They do not exist in a hierarchical relation-ship.

Does some of what your non-embodied spiritual identity is do-ing while you are in a body involve non-human activities? Yes. At times your non-embodied presence is involved in activities that have noth-ing to do with your incarnated state. These may be other adventures in other parts of the spiritual realm. Simultaneous incarnation on this or another planet may be involved. This doesn't happen frequently, but when it does occur it is often because some individuals like to chal-lenge themselves more than is normal, due to possessing more energy, or just having more derring do. Accordingly, they try balancing mul-tiple activities at once.

Other individuals are naturally more circumspect and wouldn't dream of attempting so much at once. It is all a matter of choice. Of course, those who attempt more are also more likely to crash and burn. It is certainly possible to screw up a life by not giving it suffi-cient attention because you're focused on something else. But those who fall over also tend to have a greater propensity than is usual to pick themselves up, dust off, and carry on.

This question has elucidated a somewhat long response. Nonetheless, it must be considered only an introduction to the topic, because this is another complex facet of human existence. Not everyone needs or comes to understand these matters. In part, this is because you don't need to know such things to satisfactorily live a life. More significantly, few want to know.

For those who *do* find such matters intriguing, more information is released on a need to know basis. As you dig into the circumstances of your life, and as you enter into your own awareness, you will find you lack the knowledge you need to understand what is happening to you and in you. At that time, more knowledge will become available. As is said, knock and the door will be opened. And as we keep repeating, it is entirely over to you what you learn and how far your personal store of wisdom expands.

Question 21

Will meditation initiate our next evolutionary advance?

Some people think the next phase of our evolution will involve expanding human consciousness. They've called this process noogenesis. It involves our intellectual, cultural and psychological development. But will noogenesis also be biological? You've said our spiritual development hinges on raising the vibrational quality of our awareness. I'm wondering if changes to our cognitive system will occur as we eliminate our species' fear-based thinking and feeling, making noogenesis also biological. You commented that extra-terrestrial species have very different configurations, that in some their electromagnetic aspects dominate the electrophysical. Is this where humanity is headed? And will meditation help? Will meditation initiate our next evolutionary advance?

THE GUIDES RESPOND:

No one knows what the human species will evolve into. Emergent processes certainly remain active in the human species, as they do across the universe. It is possible that capabilities latent in the human species, which currently just a few people draw on—for which they are labelled strange, or worse—may one day be accessed universally. Then intuitive abilities like insight and telepathy could become the norm.

On the other hand, it is also possible that humanity will initiate a planetwide ecological catastrophe, as a consequence of which it will radically reduce its numbers, or even make itself extinct. Naturalists have observed that species which over-populate their ecological niches run out of resources and frequently die off. We're not saying this will happen to humanity, or even that it is probable. But it is possible.

So, to address the question, while it often seems we denigrate the human brain and its cognitive capacity due to it being insufficient to access spiritual level expertise, it is also the case that the human brain possesses capacities which have not yet been tapped by the species as a whole. To that extent we not only answer, yes, the general concept of noogenesis is valid, we assert it is already under way.

Culturally, the development of the scientific method, and the resulting shift from mythological to rational explanations for what happens, has been to humanity's advantage. However, traditional perspectives, expressed in myths and legends, were not then rendered invalid. Nor are they invalid now. The mythological and the scientific, when they are based in empirical observations and are not just fanciful tales passed on by one's favorite aunt or professor, offer what are really just two different cultural perspectives on multi-dimensional reality.

Psychological evolution is another matter. In general, the scientific community resists the position that human psychology involves genetically inherited, socially conditioned *and* past life factors. Our view is that only when a reincarnational level is added will human psychological makeup be fully understood. Nonetheless, progress is being made, with a handful of researchers advancing human knowledge via depth psychology. Psychological understanding is a long way behind scientific understanding, because far fewer resources have been devoted to psychological research. Nonetheless, progress is taking place, to the extent that today psychological knowledge may be considered to be adding to human noogenesis.

As the question noted, overcoming fear is a crucial factor. Fear gives rise to senseless violence and prevents rational cooperation. It is also fuelling humanity's greed, which is exploiting entire populations and decimating the planet. When greed and fear link up, as it does in the fear of missing out, the result is catastrophic. We would say that, as the human world currently functions, greed and fear are the two primary forces actively working against noogenesis. The passive contributor is ignorance, another facet of fear, which encourages people not to ask questions, not to address the reality of their life, and not to confront what is going poorly in the world. People fear finding out that things are much worse than they suspect, so they don't look. Instead they do something much easier, which is to draw their own attention away from themselves and the world by projecting their fears onto others. Thus does ignorance fuelled by fear become the third major factor that is undermining human noogenesis.

The question was asked, what will happen once fear is eliminated from human functioning? If this happened—because we don't know the future we aren't saying it definitely will happen, we're just going along here with the possibility that it could—then a reconfiguration of the human brain's cognitive system would certainly result. Currently, human interactions involve old reptilian brain functions that evolved in prehistoric times, when human beings were regularly the prey of carnivores. At that time a fear trigger was needed to survive. Fear sparked a rush of adrenaline that resulted in the survival behaviours of fight or flight. If humanity as a whole eliminated fear from its psychological makeup, then their advanced mammalian brain would be unshackled from their old reptilian brain. Entirely new relationships could then be forged within the human brain's cognitive system, including becoming much more open to input from the spiritual self. Then the everyday human mind would automatically involve not just physical, emotional and intellectual input, but also spiritual input. Clearly, this would be a major evolutionary advance.

Neurologists have observed that the human brain is underutilised. Overcoming fear would enable more of the brain's capacity to be drawn on. Daily interactions tend to drag an individual's awareness down into self-defensive, fear-based scenarios, and so keep it involved in the low-level, coarse energies that flow from the old brain. These coarse energies then flood the cognitive system, leaving fear as a dominant driver. In contrast, the kind of evolution we are proposing involves human beings utilising, on a daily basis, higher and subtler forms of communication. For this to occur awareness needs to energetically rise above the old brain's instinctive drives. Once fears drop off, other parts of the brain can then come into play, the brain's under-utilised parts becoming active and its higher capacities engaged.

Related to this, biologists have noticed that human chromosomes contain much DNA that isn't active. They have labelled this junk DNA. The label is unfortunate. It will be corrected over time. We note that genes don't always activate automatically. Genes need to be switched on, just as they can also be switched off. Epigenetic factors, existing outside the genes, do much of the switching. These factors include environmental impacts and an individual's sustained emotional states.

To take this whole concept a big step forwards, if humanity as a whole overcame fear, disconnected awareness from the old brain's instinctive fear drivers, and as a result rewired its cognitive system, then genes that are currently inactive would become active and humanity would make a significant advance in its physical evolution. This involves emergent factors already present within human DNA, to which we referred earlier.

We observe that humanity's DNA has been adjusted in the past. Most significantly, this occurred when the brain of homo sapiens was increased from the size it inherited from its smaller brained predecessors, homo habilis and so on. The adjustment was made so human beings could lead more cognitively and emotionally complex lives, enabling the spiritual identities who entered them to have comparatively richer life experiences.

There is nothing inherently wrong or unethical about genetic engineering. As we just observed, it has happened to humanity in the past, and it is currently practised throughout the universe. Human scientists are still in the early stages of understanding what is involved. A major stumbling block, currently inhibiting progress, is that scientists don't appreciate the role the electromagnetic level plays in genetic engineering. When a foetus is in the womb, its cells not only multiply, but their growth conforms to an electromagnetic template. This template is part of the energetic envelope. The energetic template provides a pattern that directs the cells as they form the growing body. Cells respond to the template, with some becoming muscle cells, others nerve cells, others forming organs, and so on. As a result, when the new foetus starts growing, its cells follow the growth template provided by its energetic envelope.

Accordingly, when anyone engages in genetic engineering, it isn't enough to just alter the genes. The energetic envelope also needs adjusting. If there is no adjustment on the energetic level, then the changes to the DNA will not be carried by progeny permanently. Scientists have discovered this in the case of fruit flies. They can engineer the genes, but the changes don't hold across generations. The engineered flies' descendents eventually revert back to the original pre-engineered bodily form. Innumerable non-human species understand this, and carry out sophisticated genetic engineering that permanently change a species. This includes many species that have engineered their own DNA.

Will human scientists one day engineer human DNA to facilitate the evolution of the human species? It is possible. Will spiritual identities effect changes to help humanity evolve? Not necessarily, but it is also possible. Everything hinges on whether human beings can take the crucial step of changing their culture and psychology. If humanity doesn't do so, no significant evolutionary advance is possible.

The question was asked if meditation can help your evolution. It most definitely can. No matter what everyone around you is or is not doing, you can initiate your own noogenesis. It is entirely possible for you, during this life, to disconnect your cognitive system from its old brain fear-based instinctive behaviours. It is possible for you to change your own psychological make-up and behaviours. You can also change the cultural values you live by. You can take your own personal big evolutionary step. Meditation contributes to that in the many ways we have already discussed.

Of course, meditation is not the only activity that will help your personal noogenesis. What is also required is facing up to your fears, addressing your self-limiting behaviours, overcoming negative attitudes and emotions, and opening your mind to accommodate spiritual perspectives. Meditation is just one tool in your self-transformation kit. It may not even be the most useful tool. You need to discover for yourself, in the context of your life, how meditation best stimulates growth and what role it may usefully play in your self-transformation.

Will humanity eventually evolve to match what many other species throughout the multiverse have achieved? Specifically, will humanity evolve to a physical state in which their body is like fog suspended in the electrophysical? To answer this question, it is worth opening out the context.

Elsewhere we have said that each life is an experiment in consciousness. You set up the conditions for a life, select a body and culture, choose positive and negative character traits, decide who you will meet, then enter the body and live the life that results. You have a plan, but nothing is set in stone. All lives are an experiment. The elements are assembled then allowed to combine or repel one another in whichever ways they do.

In the same sense, the human species is an experiment. Life on this planet began with single-celled amoeba. Various life forms then evolved, utilising the emergent factors embedded in biological life and, via some judicious genetic engineering, carried out by those who were trained to do so. Life eventually blossomed into the stunning varieties of flora and fauna that currently occupy ecological niches across the planet. In this sense, the human species is just one among innumerable life forms that exist here. It just happens that humanity possesses adaptive capabilities not available to other species, capabilities that have led to it becoming a dominant species.

The question is, will life on this planet keep evolving? In particular, will humanity evolve to a higher level? Another way of asking this is: will the human experiment in consciousness continue, or will it be terminated—most likely through self-extermination?

This is a key question. It is possible that humanity will evolve to a very different balance of the electrophysical, electromagnetic and electrospiritual than currently applies. But to do this human beings as a species need to make fundamental changes to the way they function on this planet. What adds urgency to answering this question is that the planet's biosphere is reaching a tipping point. If nothing is changed soon, if the human species doesn't learn to control its greed and fear and to cease hiding in ignorance, not just the human species, but the planet as a whole, is headed for a spectacular crash.

It may be that a radical self-adjustment of population, to a billion or fewer, would be advantageous to humanity and its continued evolution. That level of adjustment would certainly benefit the planet and every other species. With a radically smaller human population it may also become feasible to establish a less greedy, fear-driven culture. Optimally, this would be achieved in such a way that the current levels of knowledge and technology remain functional, enabling the human species to integrate science and spirituality and so continue evolving to a level potentially far beyond what humanity currently conceives.

We are aware that what we have just suggested resembles what has been written about in speculative science fiction. We do not know precisely what will happen. However, having learned what happened to other species on other planets, our suggestion is a scenario that would allow humanity to initiate its next major evolutionary advance. At this stage, it is no more than educated speculation on our part. We reiterate, something quite different could occur. But this is a feasible future possibility.

Everything starts with you and what you do now. We leave you with that thought. Think about it. Meditate on it. Share it with others. Until our next set of communications, we wish you well.